Fishing
Vermont's
Streams
&
Lakes

Fishing Vermont's Streams & Lakes

A Guide to the Green Mountain State's Best Trout & Bass Waters

By Peter F. Cammann

with photographs by the author

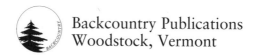
Backcountry Publications
Woodstock, Vermont

An Invitation to the Reader

With time, access points may change, and road numbers, signs, and land-marks referred to in this book may be altered. If you find that such changes have occurred near the streams described in this book, please let the author and publisher know, so that corrections may be made in future editions. Other comments and suggestions are also welcome. Address all correspondence to:

Fishing Editor
Backcountry Publications
P.O. Box 175
Woodstock, Vermont 05091

Library of Congress Cataloging-in-Publication Data
Cammann, Peter F., 1957–
        Fishing Vermont's streams & lakes: a guide to the Green Mountain State's best trout & bass waters / by Peter F. Cammann.
            p.   cm.
        Includes index.
        ISBN 0-88150-239-1
            1. Fishing—Vermont.   2. Trout fishing—Vermont.   3. Bass fishing—Vermont.   I. Title.   II. Title: Fishing Vermont's streams and lakes.
        SH555.C36   1992
        799. 1'755—dc20   92-26300
                                                                    CIP

10   9   8   7   6   5   4   3   2   1

Published by Backcountry Publications
A division of The Countryman Press, Inc.
P.O. Box 175, Woodstock, Vermont 05091

Cover design by Donna Wohlfarth
Text design by Rachel Kahn
Maps by Richard Widhu © 1992
Photographs by Peter F. Cammann

Printed in the United States of America on recycled paper

DEDICATION

To Lauren, my favorite fishing partner.

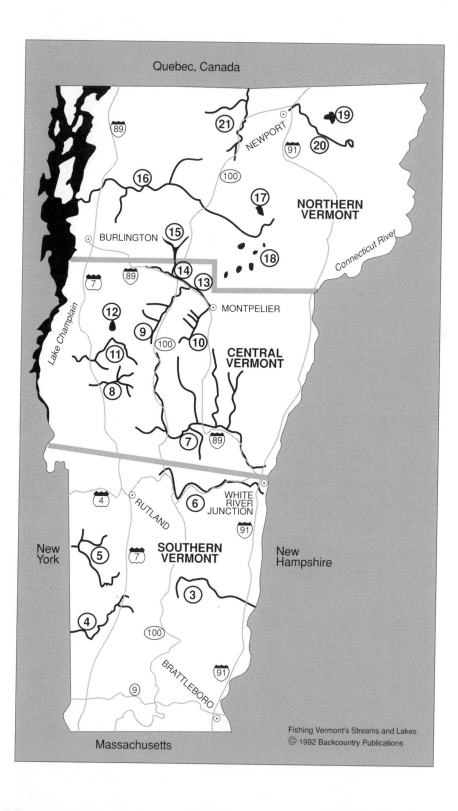

Quebec, Canada

NORTHERN VERMONT

NEWPORT

BURLINGTON

Connecticut River

MONTPELIER

CENTRAL VERMONT

Lake Champlain

WHITE RIVER JUNCTION

RUTLAND

New York

SOUTHERN VERMONT

New Hampshire

BRATTLEBORO

Massachusetts

Fishing Vermont's Streams and Lakes
© 1992 Backcountry Publications

Contents

Acknowledgments   9
1 Introduction   13
2 Fishing Tactics and Equipment   20

SECTION ONE: SOUTHERN VERMONT

3 The Williams River   29
4 The Batten Kill River   35
5 The Mettawee River   43
6 The Ottauquechee River   51

SECTION TWO: CENTRAL VERMONT

7 The White River   62
8 Ripton Gorge and The Middlebury River   73
9 The Mad River   81
10 The Dog River   91
11 The New Haven River   101
12 Winona Lake (Bristol Pond)   107
13 The Winooski River   117
14 The Little River   125

SECTION THREE: NORTHERN VERMONT

15 The Waterbury Reservoir   135
16 The Lamoille River   145
17 Caspian Lake   153
18 The Woodbury/Calais Lake Region   161
19 Seymour Lake   169
20 The Clyde River   175
21 The Missisquoi River   185
22 Beaver Pond Brookies   191

Index   199

ACKNOWLEDGMENTS

A friend of mine told me with great sympathy in his voice upon hearing that I had just completed this guidebook, "No one should ever have to write a book alone. It's just too damned hard." Fortunately, I did not have to go this one on my own; I had lots of help.

I needed an enormous amount of technical data regarding the fish populations of the rivers, lakes, and ponds I wanted to discuss in this book. To that end, I contacted the folks at the Vermont Fish and Wildlife Department. All of them were ready and willing to offer me the benefit of their experience, and I want to thank them for their patience and good humor in coping with my constant demands. I would especially like to note Rod Wentworth, Ken Cox, Dave Callum, Chet Mackenzie, Phil Wightman, John Claussen, and Rich Kirn. I would also like to thank Peter Baranco of the Department of Environmental Conservation for helping me with the history of the Waterbury Reservoir.

Of course the folks at Backcountry Publications were kind, understanding, and surprisingly tolerant of me during the preparation of this manuscript. God only knows how much sleep poor Carl Taylor lost wondering if I was ever going to get it all done in time! Special thanks go to Castle Freeman and Eric Bauer for their editing services and to my wife Lauren for helping to fine-tune the manuscript.

I also must express my sincere appreciation to the many guides who helped by offering me the benefit of their years of experience on the pieces of water described in this book. I would like to list them now, with their addresses, so that you, the reader, will be able to take advantage of the enormous knowledge they command.

Deane Wheeler
89 Young Street
Newport, VT 05855
(802) 334-2045

John Gospodarek
P.O. Box 121
East Calais, VT 05650
(802) 456-1424

Michael Olden
HCR 61, Box 8
Newport, VT 05855
(802) 334-5525

Louis Kircher
R.R. 1, Box 210
Greensboro Bend, VT 05842
(802) 533-7063

Wesley Carkin
Box 132
Manchester, VT 05255
(802) 362-4340

David Deen
R.F.D. 3, Box 800
Putney, VT 05346
(802) 869-3116

Martin Banak
Box 721
Quechee, VT 05059
(802) 295-7620

William Knight
P.O. Box 141
Stowe, VT 05672
(802) 253-4556

Fishing Vermont's Streams & Lakes

1

Introduction

When I was a kid, I learned how to fish out of the pond behind our house. It was a big piece of water, and it stretched behind lots of other people's houses. It was even large enough for the town to build a small one-lane bridge across its narrowest point. The bridge was a prime fishing spot, and you could always find children, mothers, and grown men fishing from it during the summer months. We caught white perch and eels there on long cane rods with worms and shiners as our baits.

One day, when I was about eight years old, I walked along the banks of the pond across several neighbors' yards to the bridge to do some fishing. As I first spotted the bridge, I noticed it was deserted except for an old man who was casting his line from the bridge's far corner into a reedy part of the pond. As I drew nearer, I could see him stand and stretch once or twice. There was no wind on the water, and the sun felt warm on my small shoulders.

When I got up to the bridge, I selected a spot right in the center of the far side, away from the only other angler present, where the light current moved under the pilings. I baited my hook, pitched out the line, and waited. Nothing happened. After a half-hour I looked over to the other side. The old man was pulling out a nice-sized perch. I brought in my line, laid the pole on the edge of the bridge, and walked over to him. As I watched him gently take the fish off the line, I spoke up.

"Excuse me," I asked, "but why are you fishing all the way over in that corner? The water's not very deep there, and the whole bridge is free."

The old man never looked up at me. He reached down into the water to pull up his stringer, and when he did I almost fell down with surprise. His stringer had at least a hundred perch on it!

"It's where the fish are," he replied simply as he fixed the new perch he had just caught onto the stringer and dropped it into the pond. "There's plenty of 'em right next to me; why don't you come over?"

That was the first time I was ever guided on a fishing trip, and it taught me the value of fishing with someone who knew "where the fish are." This book is my own effort to help you find the fish in Vermont's streams, lakes, and ponds.

MAPS

Before you begin to pore over the twenty-odd locations I have picked for your consideration, I have a few suggestions on how to make the most of your fishing trip to Vermont. The first is that you arm yourself with a good, accurate road atlas of the state. I like the *Vermont Road Atlas and Guide* published by Northern Cartographic of Burlington, Vermont, although the famous *Vermont Gazetteer* by David DeLorme & Company of Yarmouth, Maine, is equally good. Both of these atlases provide detailed drawings of Vermont's many town and state roads and their proximity to rivers, lakes, and other smaller waterways.

I suggest you use my book as a basic guide to the various pieces of trout, salmon, and bass water I describe and use the atlas as your blueprint for each fishing trip you take. The best way to find fish is to go places where people are scarce. Most of the waterways discussed in this guidebook are known, to Vermonters and out-of-staters alike. Nevertheless, even though places like the Batten Kill River and the Waterbury Reservoir receive a good amount of traffic during the summer months, there are many spots on them that receive little or no fishing pressure. These are the spots you will want to fish.

When reading my descriptions of the various rivers selected for this book, have your atlas within easy reach. When I tell you about a given mile or so of a river, look at the atlas and see if you can find the area I am discussing. Then look for a length of that river that winds a good distance away from the roadway running alongside it. One thing I have learned is that while most weekend anglers love their sport, they are often unwilling to walk more than a few dozen yards from the easiest access point to the piece of water they choose to fish. Therefore places out of sight of the main road, hidden behind a long field and a stand of trees, produce the best fishing.

GUIDES

Another aid you may wish to employ when venturing into Vermont's many trout streams and bass ponds is a fishing guide. In writing this book, I spoke with almost twenty different guides about their work and the waters they guide to. As a fishing guide, I pride myself on my ability to show newcomers to my region the waters where I live and work. But in order to supply you with the most accurate information on those streams and lakes where I have only an amateur level of knowledge, I chose to seek out the people who, like me, are in the business of knowing the water in their areas.

I spent months interviewing guides from all over the state, and I discovered two things. First, the fishing here in Vermont is as exciting and varied as the countryside is beautiful. I traveled from my home in the Mad River Valley to the northernmost parts of the Northeast Kingdom and Seymour Lake for lake trout; to the south to the Mettawee and Batten Kill rivers, and to the great rivers of the north-central part of the state, the White and the Winooski. Vermont is a small state, but it possesses a wide variety of fishing opportunities for the angler who wishes to seek them out.

It is because Vermont offers so many types of fishing that a guide can be a good idea for the first-time visitor. I always hire a guide when I visit a new state or a foreign country and plan to do a little fishing there. After spending a day or two with an experienced guide, I find that not only have I learned about some great new fishing spots, but I also have picked up a trick or two from the guide on fishing technique which will serve me wherever I choose to fish in the future, either at home or on the road.

The second thing I learned in interviewing Vermont fishing guides for this book is that the guides, like the people of Vermont, are always willing to help an angler looking for a good piece of water to fish. Vermonters are like the people you meet anywhere. They are glad to help a polite angler find a particular place and will even occasionally tell you about a few of their own favorite fishing holes. The rule of thumb is to remember that you are a visitor when you ask for directions or for permission to cross a landowner's field to get to a promising stretch of trout stream. This courtesy is as important for the native Vermonter fishing new water on the far side of the gap from where he lives as it is for the first-time visitor.

CATCH-AND-RELEASE FISHING

A common courtesy you should observe when fishing in Vermont—or anywhere else, for that matter—is to follow the rules of catch-and-release fishing. At one time or another we have all employed the catch-and-release philosophy. Surely you can remember when you were a kid pulling up an undersized fish and with a bit of annoyance tossing it back into the water.

That is part, but not the whole story behind catch-and-release fishing. As a kid, you did not want the small fish, only the big ones. The smaller fish just got in the way. But, by throwing back the small fish, you made it possible for them to grow into larger catches for another day. You may not have been aware of it, but you were practicing a basic form of conservation.

Conservation is crucial to fishing in Vermont. If you have ever fished the state, you have probably noticed that we have some of the prettiest streams, best fishing ponds, and most productive lakes found any-where in the East. At times it may seem the fishing in Vermont is so good that the huge supply of fun and food can never run out. That is an unfortunate misconception. More of us fish today in America than at any other time in our history. It is estimated that one out of four of us goes fishing each year, and that accounts for over 60 million people nationwide. With more than 100,000 Vermonters out on the water each season, plus all those out-of-state visitors who come to enjoy the fishing here, a lot of pressure comes to bear on our resources.

That is why releasing most of our daily catch makes good sense. Sure, eating a fish taken from the water only hours before is a rare pleasure as well as one of the great rewards of fishing. However, we have to remember that if we all keep too many fish each season, the supply will suffer, as will the future of fishing in Vermont.

So the next time you are having one of those tremendous days out on the water and you have one or two good fish in your creel for dinner already, why not release the ones you catch after that? Just be careful to handle the fish gently, always making sure your hands are wetted down to prevent injury to it. If possible, carry a pair of forceps and remove the hook from the fish's mouth without touching it at all. Let your fish go in calm water, and always make sure any fish to be released is healthy and uninjured. Any sign of bleeding around the gills is a sure indication that the fish is hurt and will probably not survive. If necessary, revive your fish gently in the water by holding its tail and slowly moving the fish back and forth in the water to help force extra oxygen through the gills. When the fish is ready to swim, it will thrash in your hand, and you can let it go.

PHOTOGRAPHY TIPS

In the next chapter I discuss the various techniques and equipment you will want to employ on your fishing trips in Vermont. But before I get into that, I would like to offer a quick word about a much-misunderstood bit of gear. One of the most neglected pieces of equipment we anglers bring along when we go fishing is a camera.

We all have photos of our favorite fishing trips: the one where you took a party boat out on Lake Champlain for lakers, that weekend canoeing trip on Seymour for brown trout, or even the time you went out after work one day in the early spring on the Winooski and caught a nice big rainbow. The problem is, most of us take the exact same photo every time we go out. You know the one: a huge fish in the arms of a grinning angler.

I know it is important to have a picture that records the daily catch, but does every roll of film we take out on the water have to be restricted to this one type of shot? There is a lot going on out on the water, and most of us are missing it when we photograph our fishing trips.

Try taking pictures of your fishing buddies as they battle their catch. Do not limit this to close-ups of your friends grimacing as the fish pulls out some hard-fought line. Train your lens out on the water when the fish gets in range, and try to shoot it as it jumps. This is a tough shot to make, but with a little practice you can do it. Also, if you are traveling with a large enough group, pull alongside and get some action photos of the folks in the boat nearest to you. This is an unusual camera angle and provides some nice perspective for your friends back home on what it really felt like to be out there that day.

Take photos of your surroundings. Normally, fish live in very pretty places. You also might try photographing the other wildlife you encounter: deer, waterfowl, and small game. They too are part of the whole experience of fishing, and in photographing them you will learn a lot about how they interact with the water, the fish, and each other.

Streamside anglers should take photos of their fishing buddies from as many angles as possible. Do not limit yourself to following along from downstream and shooting your friends from the same side. Get up on a high bank, or shoot from the opposite shoreline to get in as much of the natural surroundings as you can. You will find that varied camera angles greatly enhance your pictures and your ability to tell the story of your trip once you get home.

SCOPE OF THIS BOOK

Primarily because I wish this book to concentrate on the smaller pieces of water in the state, I have omitted two major Vermont fisheries. I have not written about Lake Champlain, Vermont's largest fishery, because I figure that a body of water which takes up 278,400 acres should be dealt with in its own book at a later date. For the same reason, you will not read much here about the Connecticut River, except for those places along it where rivers dealt with in this book feed in. Lake Champlain and the Connecticut are two fabulous places to go fishing, and I hope you decide to explore them, even though I have not undertaken here to supply you with much information on them.

VERMONT FISHING SEASONS AND REGULATIONS

One final note: as this book deals primarily with the trout and bass of Vermont, I should advise you of the state's open-season laws. Trout fishing is permitted from the second Saturday in April through the last Sunday in October. There is a catch-and-release season for bass prior to the regular one, which begins on the second Saturday in June and ends on the last day in November. You may fish for bass from the first Saturday in April too, however you must release all of the fish you catch before the official opening date in June.

For a copy of the Vermont Digest of Fish and Wildlife Laws, or to purchase a fishing license through the mail, write to:

> Vermont Fish and Wildlife
> 103 South Main Street
> Waterbury, VT 05676

or call (802) 244-7331.

2

Fishing Tactics and Equipment

Vermont offers the angler a great variety of opportunities and challenges. The opportunities are here to fish for some of the most exciting
freshwater game fish in the world. Landlocked salmon; smallmouth
bass; northern pike; rainbow, brook, brown, and lake trout all thrive
in Vermont's many lakes, streams, and ponds. The challenges lie in
how you, the angler, choose to pursue these species.

I have chosen to stress equipment and tactics designed for fly-fishing
in this book, although I also have included some information for those
who fish with light spinning tackle and artificial lures. (In Chapter 12,
Winona Lake, you will find additional information on spin-fishing
tactics—especially those effective with northern pike.) Artificial flies
and lures are important to the scope of this guidebook, as their use
offers the best opportunities for catch-and-release fishing. In the
introduction I stressed that you should limit the number of fish you
keep each day. I hope that, in using the information on the various
fishing spots discussed in the following chapters, you will take this
point to heart and endeavor to use either flies or, at least, artificial
spinning lures.

FLIES AND OTHER LURES

The reason why artificials help a catch-and-release strategy is fascinat-
ing in itself. Fish have very highly developed senses of smell, sight, and

hearing. Anyone who has blundered too quickly onto a piece of water and watched helplessly as several good-sized fish moved rapidly out of the area can attest to their acute hearing and sight. Similarly, anglers who carelessly forget to wash their hands after applying insect repellent rarely are successful, as the fish smell the chemicals on the lure or fly that is next handled by the angler.

But how aware are you of the fish's sense of taste? Obviously, fish must taste what they feed on; otherwise we would catch every trout or bass by gut-hooking it with our flies and lures. As you know, fish will spit out these artificial baits almost the instant they strike at them. The reason is simply that these things taste wrong to the fish, and they will immediately recognize and reject what isn't really food for them.

If we take a trout as an example, it will breathe in the fly and taste the water surrounding it. If it tastes like what the fish normally associates with a living insect, it will swallow the fly and move on. However, should the trout taste brass, feathers, or fur, it will breathe the fly out, back into the water, and retreat. This entire process takes perhaps a half a second, and within that small time frame there is still a wide margin of error in the fish's favor. If the angler is a split-second too quick in setting the hook, the fly will be yanked out of the fish's mouth before it has even had a chance to taste it. On the other hand, a late strike by the angler will provide the fish with the split-second it needs to begin rejecting the fly, causing the hook to set in the fleshy outer part of the mouth, if it sets at all. This will allow the fish to eventually tear the hook away and escape while the agitated angler watches from the shore.

On a fishing trip to the Dog River with two clients, I was asked to demonstrate how to fish a long, deep pool with a streamer. There was no movement on the water, but I had spotted two very large, 3- to 4-pound brown trout there several weeks before. I tied on a Royal Coachman streamer and began casting to the opposite shore, at a large clump of partially submerged wood and debris. I was working on explaining how to retrieve the streamer so that it looks like a wounded minnow when the big brown hit. I struck back just a fraction of a second too late. I did hook the fish, but after it had completed its swirling attack and headed upstream away from me, the hook popped harmlessly out of the brown's mouth and it was gone.

My two clients were astounded. One of them asked how I had lost the fish. Had my line broken? Had the knot come undone? The streamer was still attached to the leader, and I continued my casting lesson after briefly explaining how this beautiful trophy had escaped. I never really mind losing a good fish in this way; such defeats sort of remind me of the old-time shoot-outs in the American West. Two gunslingers square off against each other, and only the fastest and sharpest survives. When a fish beats you purely by speed and not due to some minute error in the preparation of your tackle, it is a great feeling. You have competed with the best and lost. It remains for you to improve your skills for the next showdown.

Getting back to the use of artificials, you can see now how it helps the angler employ a catch-and-release strategy. The fish is on equal footing with the angler and is not likely to inhale your fly or lure so deeply as to cause itself internal damage. Still, there are those rare cases of the fish injuring itself during the fight. Occasionally, a feeding fish will swallow an artificial fly deeply enough that the hook comes into contact with the gills as you fight it. The rubbing of the hook against these vital organs will often cause a fatal injury. This is exhibited by bleeding of the gills, a sure sign that the fish will soon die. While I urge all of you to release fish you catch, this is one time when you must take it. Releasing a dead or dying fish into the water is not only a cruel way to deal with so proud an adversary, it is also wasteful.

FISHING FROM A CANOE

This brings up another important point: respect for wildlife and the environment. I know most of you would no more waste an injured fish than you would go out fishing in a lightning storm. Simple logic dictates that you act responsibly when out on the water. However, respect for the environment also inspires another feature of this book's approach: I discuss fishing strategies of streamside and canoe guides far more than those of guides who use motorboats for fishing. You see, not only is a canoe strategy more sound for the environment, it also simply makes better sense.

Canoes allow you to move soundlessly through the water, which in turn means you can sneak up on feeding fish effectively. In 1985 I wrote an article for a magazine about canoeing the ocean waters near Buzzard's Bay in Massachusetts. I used to live right on Apponagansett

Bay, in the town of South Dartmouth, where I worked as a newspaper reporter. Every day during the summer I would leave the newspaper office and walk down to the beach where I used to leave my canoe. I would pack up my fly rod and some spinning gear and launch the canoe into the quiet waters of the harbor to look for the migrating bluefish. While bluefish are not particularly selective, they are extremely sensitive to sound and will often abandon a school of baitfish should they hear the rumble of an outboard motor. On the other hand, I discovered that I could move my canoe right on top of a school of feeding bluefish without ever disturbing them. From my vantage point I would make short casts with a streamer to the fish as they chased the bait along the surface. Sometimes these big fish, which can weigh well over 20 pounds, would actually brush up against my canoe as they cornered the fleeing baitfish.

The same principle works when applied to bass, trout, northern pike, or any other freshwater game fish. If you can position your canoe

A setup of a four- to eight-weight rod and line with a well-built reel will serve you well anywhere you fish in Vermont.

quietly and carefully, you can dramatically reduce the length of your cast to rising fish. Often you will be able to spot fish in your vicinity by looking down into the water while wearing a pair of polarized sunglasses. You may have to switch to a weighted fly line and take a long, silent swing through this same area to get those deeper-swimming fish to bite, but you will be able to locate them nonetheless.

As trout have very highly developed senses of hearing and sight, a quiet approach is vital either by canoe or by foot. Through refraction of light, trout's field of view above water is nearly doubled, and they can see almost 330 degrees around them, with the only real blind spot being the space directly behind. This is why you will observe trout facing upstream when they hold in the current of a river. In this way they can most effectively guard against the intrusion of predators while they keep an eye out for food washing into their territory via the river flow. However, a trout's vision reaches its limit at roughly thirty feet, and to warn it of more distant objects it will rely on its acute sense of hearing.

Sound travels better in water than it does in the air because the waves produced by any given object are better conducted through the denser of the two mediums. This is why a fish will hear you approach well before you have swung into its field of view—and why it is easier to sneak up on a fish from downstream than upstream. The sound waves you create by moving through the water are speeded toward the waiting fish by the river's current if you move downstream, but they are actually pushed away from the fish if you approach by moving upstream.

On flat water, like a slow-moving pool in a river or the surface of a pond or a lake, sound travels at a constant rate of speed. Furthermore, all the sound you produce moves in all directions at the same time, making your efforts at approaching fish far more difficult. It is therefore very important for you to minimize your movements while fishing calm water. One guide I know, William Knight of William's Canoe Fishing, covers the bottom of his canoes with rugs so as to muffle the noise made by himself and his clients as they paddle, change gear, and move about in the canoe. This is a simple preventive measure, but one which gives the angler a distinct advantage when fishing slow-moving or flat water.

Fishing by canoe also allows you a better opportunity to observe the wildlife that lives along the shores of Vermont's waters. I have seen moose, deer, bear, mink, otter, beaver, and bobcat while fishing either from the shore or by canoe, something I doubt many motorboat enthusiasts can claim.

EQUIPMENT

The equipment which is best suited to fishing in the waters to be discussed runs a fairly full gamut. As each piece of water is reviewed, I will make recommendations; however, here are a few ideas about what you might want to bring along.

For fly rods, I would use anything in the 3 to 6 weights. I have a personal preference for 3- and 4-weight rods with a soft-action tip in a 7- to 7½-foot length. However, there are plenty of places like the Clyde River or Seymour Lake where you are going to want something quite a bit heavier. While we are on this subject, I would keep a wide variety of tippet material, say in the 6X to 3X range. There will be times when you can get away with 7X tippets, but just as many occasions where you will want the heavier 3X and even 2X material.

Spin-anglers can really enjoy fishing in Vermont, as you can bring almost anything along and eventually find water where it is applicable. Bait-casting reels for spinnerbaits and open-face reels for jigs, spoons, and spinners are a must, as you are going to be fishing for bass as well as trout. But remember to keep your line reasonably light. I do not believe you will need to use anything over 6-pound test, except for those locations where you are likely to hook into landlocked salmon. These fish can really tear you up. Stick to short rods, never over 5½ feet, as Vermont streams are notorious for their many overhangs and tight spots.

SECTION ONE

SOUTHERN VERMONT

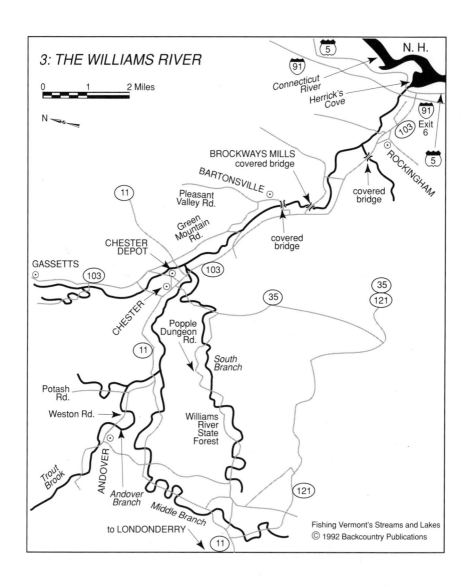

3: THE WILLIAMS RIVER

0   1   2 Miles

N

N. H.

5

91

Connecticut River

Herrick's Cove

91

Exit 6

103

5

ROCKINGHAM

BROCKWAYS MILLS
covered bridge

BARTONSVILLE

covered bridge

11

Pleasant Valley Rd.

Green Mountain Rd.

covered bridge

CHESTER DEPOT

GASSETTS

103

103

35

121

CHESTER

35

Popple Dungeon Rd.

South Branch

11

Potash Rd.

Williams River State Forest

Weston Rd.

Trout Brook

ANDOVER

121

Andover Branch

Middle Branch

to LONDONDERRY

11

Fishing Vermont's Streams and Lakes
© 1992 Backcountry Publications

3

The Williams River

The main stem of the Williams River makes its beginning in the town of Andover. It flows twenty-five miles through Chester and Rockingham before it empties out into the Connecticut River. This is not a large river, in fact much of it is very tough to fish during the midsummer months when the air temperatures hit the high eighties. However, one section of the Williams supports smallmouth bass, rock bass, brook trout, and rainbows. This is where we are going to concentrate our efforts in this chapter.

First though, let us take a quick look at some of the other highlights of this most unusual piece of water. Trout Brook starts in the western part of Andover and feeds into the Andover Branch near Andover village. The Andover Branch meets the Middle Branch near where Weston Road and VT 11 intersect in Chester. All this water is good for brook trout fishing, and access is reasonably good. I should also point out that the Middle Branch itself begins in Londonderry, near the intersection of VT 11 and VT 121. This stretch of water is best reached via VT 11.

The South Branch of the river winds through the Williams River State Forest in the southwestern corner of Chester and meets the main stem near Chester village. By the time this last branch enters the main stem, the Williams River is a viable fishery for brown trout as well as brookies. The main access, which has been VT 11 all along the top half of the river, now intersects with VT 103 right in Chester village.

Guide David Deen fishes a deep pool along the lower portion of the Williams River in Rockingham.

Another important landmark is the Green Mountain Railroad, which runs alongside the river from the village all the way to the Connecticut River. VT 103 only crosses the river once between Chester Depot and the Connecticut, just north of the village. All your best accesses will be along the river's southern bank, if you choose to follow the highway south.

There is another alternative, however: go north on VT 103 and follow the highway up to the village of Gassetts. Here VT 103 does cross the main stem of the river. You will also find several small roads that cross the river running off the highway. One good road to follow south is the Green Mountain Road, which runs from Chester Depot to Bartonsville where it hits Pleasant Valley Road. This small road heads into Bartonsville village, and eventually, if you keep following it to the south, it goes through a covered bridge which spans the Williams River.

There are three covered bridges that pass over the Williams. The one farthest upstream is the one near Bartonsville. The next as you head downstream is at Brockway Mills. Between this bridge and Chester village is where most of the state Fish and Wildlife Department stocking efforts take place.

The state has been stocking the river from Brockway Mills upstream with rainbows, browns, and brook trout. Since 1981 the Middle Branch and the South Branch have received thousands of brook trout, as has the section of the main stem which runs from Chester village upstream to Gassetts. It is important to note, though, that the South Branch has received only one stocking of 5,000 brookies between 1981 and 1990. The Middle Branch received anywhere between 500 and 1,000 brook trout annually from 1981 to 1989.

The main stem, as it runs from Gassetts to Chester village, has not been stocked since 1987. In that year the state placed 900 brookies in the river. Prior to that date, the state regularly stocked between 500 and 1,000 fish annually there.

The stretch of the Williams that has received the most stocking is that portion which runs from Chester village to Brockway Mills. From 1981 to 1986 between 1,400 and 2,900 brown trout were placed in this part of the river. Stocking of rainbow trout continues as of this writing, with the numbers running between 1,000 and 2,700 each year. The rainbow stocking is actually increasing each year, which is contrary to the trend along the rest of the river. At Brockway Mills there is a hydro site and a deep gorge which prevents most of the stocked fish from ever venturing downstream. This area is truly a wild fishery and is a spectacular place to spend time with a light fly rod and your favorite assortment of nymphs, streamers, and terrestrials.

David Deen runs an Orvis-endorsed guide service out of Putney called Strictly Trout. The Orvis endorsement means that while he provides his guide services as an independent businessman, he is also under contract to the Orvis Company, and so, for example, can supply Orvis equipment to his many clients. David is experienced in guiding most of the major rivers of Vermont and has fished the Williams extensively.

I fished with David on one very hot summer day not too long ago, and he took me through the whole section which runs from Brockway Mills downstream through Herrick's Cove, a wide, beautiful area where the Connecticut and the Williams meet. We started by taking my

Mad River canoe through the cove in search of smallmouth bass.

Herrick's Cove is owned by the New England Power Company, which also owns the large hydroelectric dam downstream on the Connecticut River.

The morning we fished in the cove, the dam was not yet letting water through, and as a result the water levels were high and the fish were active. Because the cove is such a wide, flat area, you will find that when the dam is shut off fishing is actually better than when the water level starts to drop after it has been turned on. Fishing an impoundment like this cove is far different from tailwater fishing on the downstream side of a power dam. I will be discussing tailwater later on in this book, so we will concentrate here instead on fishing upstream from a dam when the turbines are turned on and off.

For a dam to make power it must force large amounts of water through its turbines. This can only happen if the river or reservoir behind it has an ample water supply. On the lower Williams and the Connecticut rivers, this volume of water is supplied by the flow of the streams. When the power company decides to flush water through the dam, the water level upstream drops dramatically. A release can leave fish in up to three feet less water than they are used to, and in a very short period of time. In Herrick's Cove, some of the shallows where bass often like to congregate can become exposed when the dam is opened, and all you will see are mud flats where once there was water.

On the morning that David and I took to the cove, the water was up, and the fishing was good. We paddled about, looking for submerged tree stumps and sunken logs to cast to. The smallmouth were everywhere and aggressively hit streamer patterns like the Royal Coachman and Woolly Bugger. They did not seem too interested in any of the popping bugs we offered them, but instead were content to attack below the surface. We did not have to fish our streamers too deep, though, only about a foot down.

The cove is very wide as it feeds into the Connecticut, and there is virtually no current when the water level is high. It is like paddling about on a small lake. There are plenty of places to pull alongside of to get out of the wind, as well. One of the best was a small island which you find right at the upstream end of the cove, near where I-91 crosses it.

There is a boat access on the north shoreline of the cove. Bass anglers will want to make use of it if they plan on launching large bass boats with power motors. Take US 5 to the point just north of the junction with VT 103. There is a sign pointing east that says: "New England Power Company Picnic Area." Follow that road to the end, and you will find the access.

After heading back upstream to where we had launched our canoe, David pointed out that the water level was beginning to drop. We stowed the canoe on top of my car and put on our waders. It was time to explore the upstream area, which makes up the river itself.

The whole area of the Williams from Brockway Mills down to just upstream from the I-91 bridge is a small but extremely beautiful stream filled with brook trout, smallmouth, and rock bass. There are about a dozen good stretches of water spread out along this four or five miles of river, but they are separated by some very long pieces of shallow water that are far less productive. However, the parts where the fish do live each take up a fairly large area, and it will take you a good deal of time to work your way through each of them.

We found that our best luck was had by drifting nymphs and streamers down through the current, sometimes weighted with a small piece of split shot. I would make short casts upstream and then let the fly drift past me. When the line began to swing around in the current, I would slowly begin to retrieve the slack. I managed to hook most of my fish in this manner.

David is a terrific nymph fisherman, and he caught several good-sized smallmouth by working his flies along the river bottom. He also likes to use a Hare's Ear, fished just above the floor of the stream. He is methodical in the way he works a pool or riffle and always came out with one more fish than I did on each piece of water we fished together. The one funny habit he has is cursing the occasional rock bass that hits his line. Like so many other anglers I have fished with, David holds these poor creatures in great disdain. As you will find out later on in the chapter on the Clyde River, I enjoy fishing for rock bass. To be sure, they are not as thrilling as the smallmouth or as glamorous as the rainbow trout. Still, a medium-sized rock bass can put up an energetic fight, especially on light fly gear. On the Williams I was using my favorite 4-weight Fenwick, and David was using a 4-weight Orvis rod. Both of us had a great time working on the 1- and 2-pound fish we found all through this stretch of the river.

We even ran across one pool which held some small rainbows. Vermont does not stock this portion of the river, but these fish were there nonetheless. They were not wild fish, though. David pointed out that the state of New Hampshire manages the Connecticut River as a rainbow fishery, and they stock thousands of these trout below the New England Power dam. The trout work their way up the fish ladders at the dam and eventually seek out the cool water of rivers like the Williams.

One final note regarding the Williams concerns the fragility of this fishery. As I pointed out, the upper and middle river can heat up quite a bit during the summer, and this does cause the fish to suffer. In the lower river, water temperatures are kept cooler by the ebb and flow of the dam and by the many small springs and brooks which feed into it. But there too the fish are in a very tough spot if too many anglers take too many fish.

I encourage you to treat the lower Williams River as a catch-and-release stretch. This magnificent piece of water, and Herrick's Cove below it, are already under enormous stress from the varying water levels from the dam and from increased pressure by bass anglers and others. If it is to continue to provide good fishing in the future, we must work now to preserve it.

4

The Batten Kill River

Perhaps the most famous piece of trout water in Vermont is the Batten Kill River; it simply must be included in any fishing guidebook of the state. So much has been written on this stream that I will save you a repeat of the rhapsodic passages of other authors. Simply put, the Batten Kill is an excellent piece of brown trout water, and for the most part it is accessible from both banks.

By any standards the Batten Kill is a small river. It begins at the intersection of the Mad Tom and Little Mad Tom brooks near East Dorset. The river here is tiny, only about eight feet wide and never much more than knee deep. Brook trout fishing is excellent, although the average size of the fish only runs to about 6 inches. Still, I have to admit that I sometimes love to pull out my smallest, 3-weight fly rod and dap the surface of this small stream with dry flies, stalking brookies.

Anglers can hike for miles along the two Mad Tom brooks or through the whole portion of the Batten Kill, which runs down into the northeastern corner of Manchester township. You will run into very few anglers and even fewer signs of any other human life. In fact, if you decide to work your way all the way up the Little Mad Tom, you find yourself at an altitude of well over two thousand feet above sea level. You may even be able to catch a glimpse of Bromley Mountain off to the east, should you venture to the top of the mountain the brook runs down.

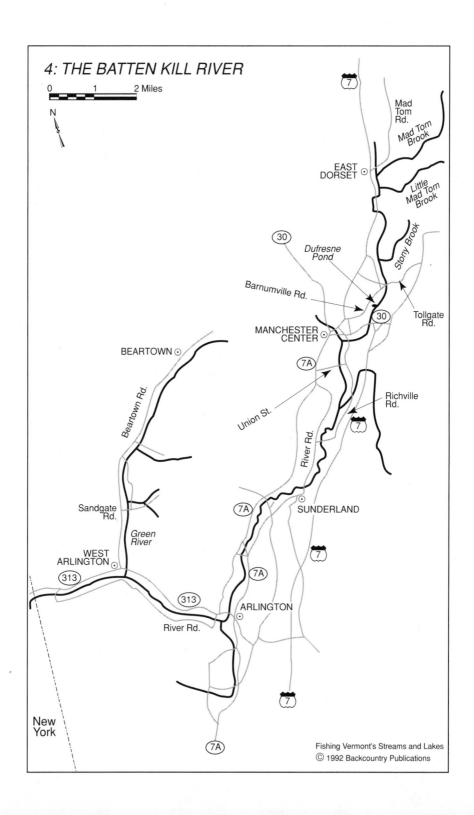

4: THE BATTEN KILL RIVER

0   1   2 Miles

N

Mad Tom Rd.

Mad Tom Brook

EAST DORSET ⊙

Little Mad Tom Brook

30

Dufresne Pond

Stony Brook

Barnumville Rd.

30

Tollgate Rd.

MANCHESTER CENTER ⊙

BEARTOWN ⊙

7A

Union St.

Richville Rd.

7

Beartown Rd.

River Rd.

Sandgate Rd.

Green River

7A

SUNDERLAND ⊙

WEST ARLINGTON ⊙

313

7

7A

313

7A

ARLINGTON ⊙

River Rd.

7

New York

7A

Fishing Vermont's Streams and Lakes
© 1992 Backcountry Publications

The water runs very clear here. Brook trout require the cleanest of water to live in, and that is why you will find so many of them. In the area of the main river which runs in between the Mad Tom and Little Mad Tom, the bottom is quite rocky and will have a few more deeper holes to fish in. The brook trout can run into the 12-inch range, and in the fall you will see a fairly good brown trout spawning run.

As the river runs downstream from the confluence with the Little Mad Tom, the average depth is about shin deep. There are more and more pools mixed in the shallower water, and the wading here is quite safe until you get to where the river passes the Chantecleer Restaurant. Not too many people bother to fish this little section of the river, and it is also where you will begin to see some of the river's famous brown trout.

All along the portion of the Batten Kill that we have discussed so far anglers can make use of a wide variety of spinning lures and flies and get good results. Wes Carkin, who guides the Batten Kill from his home in Manchester, has certain recommendations, though. Wes favors Panther Martins fished along the water's surface for best results for those who plan on spin-fishing in the river. The times I have gone fishing with Wes, he has sported a beautiful, custom-made, one-piece graphite spinning rod, and he will work the water with the Panther Martin almost to the exclusion of any other lure.

But Wes also fly-fishes, and he gave me some very good advice in this respect, as well as a warning to those who would fish this river. "If you fly-fish exclusively," he told me, "the Batten Kill can be one of the most humbling experiences of your life—or the most rewarding, should you hook up."

For the best opportunity at getting a good strike while fly-fishing the upper Batten Kill, anglers should work with Dark Hendricksons, Quill Gordons, and Muddlers during the early spring months of April and May. Wes prefers to use fairly large flies at this time of year, normally a size-14 hook. As you head into June and July, though, he recommends reducing the size of your fly to either an 18 or a 20. He also swears by the Hare's Ear, all season long.

As the river flows downstream, it becomes a bit more dangerous to wade. The whole section from where Stony Brook enters, near the golf course, down through to Dufresne Pond features a muddy bottom that can be extremely treacherous unless you are fishing with someone who knows the way. Accesses are few and far between, making fishing even harder. The up side is that there is little or no pressure on this portion of the river. Brown trout fishing here can be very good too, as the river is fairly slow-moving, which keeps these wary fish content.

Dufresne Pond is a ten-acre piece of water. Brook trout are stocked in the pond, making it the only part of the Batten Kill River which is stocked. No other part of the Batten Kill has been stocked with any species of trout since 1975. It has been managed by the state as a wild trout stream ever since. The pond is formed by a small dam which sometimes is home to the famous Orvis fly-fishing school's casting clinics. The outflow of the dam can be a very good place to fish, especially at night for brown trout. There are even a few good-sized browns in the pond itself, although the vast majority of fish are small brookies.

To give you an idea of what has been happening in terms of fish stocking in Dufresne Pond versus the Batten Kill as a whole, between 1965 and 1975 the river was stocked with almost 24,000 brown trout and around the same number of brook trout. The largest stocking year was 1965, when over 10,000 fish were placed in the river, but these numbers were tapered off over the following ten years. No brown trout have been placed in the river by the state since 1972, and stocking of other species was terminated three years later.

Dufresne Pond received 25,500 brook trout during this same eleven-year period, with 4,500 fish (the largest number during the period) being stocked in 1966. Between 1976 and 1986 the pond was stocked with between 1,000 and 2,000 brookies each year, although that number has now fallen to between 500 and 1,000 fish per year for the period of 1987 through 1990.

Where the Batten Kill winds out of the pond and toward the bridge where VT 30 crosses it, you will find some great fly-fishing water. The best time to start fishing here is after the early spring season. During April and the first part of May, the water levels can be high, making fly-fishing and wading both difficult and even a bit dangerous. The water is very flat in the section we are discussing now, so it is likely you will run into some nice-sized brown trout. You won't find too many other people fishing in here with you, either. Because all the deep pools are so open and slow-running, the fish will have ample opportunity to observe your approach. Use stealth when you first enter the water, as these fish will spook easily.

The Batten Kill winds its way through the wooded area near the New York border in Arlington, Vermont.

The next section runs from the VT 30 bridge down to where Union Street crosses the river. The area is overgrown with shrubs, tree limbs and other obstacles. While a fly-angler with a short, 6- or 6½-foot rod might be able to get under this stuff, spinning gear is more appropriate. I like using an ultralight rig like Fenwick's Legacy or their HMG rod, both of which are well under 5 feet in length. I usually match a Shimano reel like the Symetre 1000 with either of these rods. Using something this small helps me get in and around the tight spots.

There are some large brown trout lurking in the deeper sections of the river here as well as some small brook trout, in the 6-inch range. The browns will feed on the brookies, which is why Rapalas work well in here. Wes Carkin told me that he favors using a number-7 gold Rapala run along the top of the water. There is little pressure in this area from other anglers, as footing is poor along the river bottom. It is muddy, which can be hazardous if you have not fished here before.

Following is a 4-mile stretch of river that begins at the Union Street bridge and continues to the bridge where Richville Road meets River Road. In contrast to the previous two pieces of river, the wading here is excellent, and both fly- and spin-anglers should have a lot of fun wading through the knee-deep water, casting to rising fish. The fish here can be of good size, too, many of them running in the 12- to 14-inch range.

There are many twists and bends in the river, and each of these holds a good, deep pool. These holes are home to some enormous brown trout. You will want to fish them deep. The best lures to use are diving Rapalas, while the preferred flies will be heavily weighted stonefly nymphs and Woolly Buggers. A quick tip for fly-anglers: when you are fishing a piece of water like this, which features many deep pools interspersed between long, shallow runs, bring along a spare reel spool filled with sinking-tip line. You can use your double-taper or weight-forward floating line on the shallow sections. But when you get to one

Guide Wes Carkin takes time off to cast a spinning lure near his home in Manchester. Manchester is doubly blessed to be near both the Mettawee and Batten Kill rivers, two of the state's truly wild trout streams.

of those eight-foot-deep pools, switch spools and get your fly down to the bottom. By dredging your nymphs down at the very depths of a big pool, you can often get to some of those finicky browns a lot more efficiently with the sinking tip.

The best part of the river to fish for the Batten Kill's big brown trout runs between the intersection of Richville and River roads down into Arlington in the vicinity of the public recreation field. There is a canoe access on the north side of Richville Road and a good pull-out at the recreation field. This is very deep, slow-moving water, and the brown trout love it. You will also run into some decent brook trout, although this species is somewhat scarce when compared to the larger number of browns.

The paddling is easy, almost like drifting on a long, skinny pond. There are plenty of bends for you to tie up along, although with few exceptions I would not advise that you choose them as places to get out and wade. The water is deep, and the bottom is often quite muddy.

The whole section of the river from where VT 313 crosses all the way until the Batten Kill enters New York State is great fishing for medium-sized brown trout. The river widens ever so slightly here, and alternating with the gentle, flat water some gorgeous rapids and runs are to be found. The faster-moving water is a favorite of mine, as I like to swing big Muddler Minnows through the current. Brown trout seem to find these big flies irresistible, and they will often follow a streaking Muddler through the rapid and strike it only once it has passed my position and has begun to swing around in the cross current.

Access is good along this section, and you should wade it while you fish. You can get into the river along the north shore via VT 313, or you can follow the southern shore by River Road. Both will offer you many good places to step into the water.

As you enter West Arlington, about four miles before the river enters New York, there is a tributary to the Batten Kill which deserves special attention. The Green River, which starts up in Beartown, in the township of Sandgate, is a beautiful little stream filled with brook trout. It is also a staging area for fall-running brown trout. During September through October you will find lots of good-sized browns working their way up this tributary.

Fly-anglers will find that spring comes early on the Batten Kill, and so do the insect hatches. Mayflies, caddis, and stoneflies start to appear in May and will continue to hatch through most of the season. Light Cahills are also prevalent through much of June. July and August are best for terrestrials and hoppers, although you should throw a few stoneflies as well. Hellgrammites will appear too, and while I know of few anglers who use imitations of these ugly beasties, Woolly Buggers or large stonefly nymphs will do in a pinch.

5

The Mettawee River

The Mettawee is the second of two rivers discussed in this book that are currently being managed by the Vermont Fish and Wildlife Department as wild trout streams. This designation was made in 1972, and since that date no trout have been stocked in this river. A survey of the Mettawee completed shortly after this designation was made offers some interesting insights into the factors which led state Fish and Wildlife officials to "turn this one loose."

During August of 1973, 1,650 feet of the Mettawee were the subject of an electrofishing survey. A total of 155 trout were counted during the survey, of which 98 were browns, 42 rainbows and 15 were brookies. What was dramatic about this group of fish was that 60 percent of the rainbows and 56 percent of the brown trout were at least a year old. Twenty-six percent of all of the brown trout were actually over two years old. Given that the study indicated a ratio of one trout for every eleven feet of river and that these trout were living as long as they were, it was obvious that the Mettawee was a most healthy stretch of trout water.

Today the Mettawee remains one of the finer rivers in the state. It's a small river, most of it is less than 20 feet wide as it flows northwestward through the fields and woods of southwestern Vermont for seventeen miles and into New York State. However, it holds some very large trout and some of the most beautiful sights you are apt to encounter on any fishing trip in the Green Mountain State. It could be argued that the

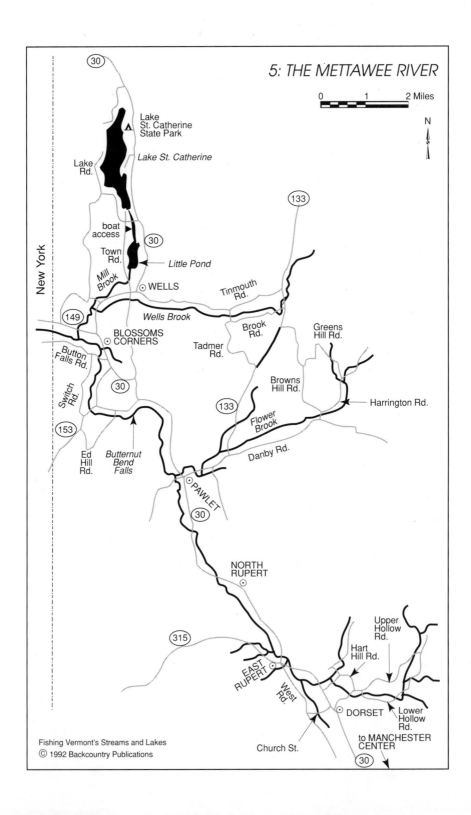

5: THE METTAWEE RIVER

0   1   2 Miles

N

Lake St. Catherine State Park

Lake St. Catherine

Lake Rd.

boat access

Town Rd.

Little Pond

Mill Brook

WELLS

Tinmouth Rd.

Wells Brook

BLOSSOMS CORNERS

Brook Rd.

Greens Hill Rd.

Tadmer Rd.

Button Falls Rd.

Switch Rd.

Browns Hill Rd.

Harrington Rd.

Flower Brook

Ed Hill Rd.

Butternut Bend Falls

Danby Rd.

PAWLET

NORTH RUPERT

Upper Hollow Rd.

Hart Hill Rd.

EAST RUPERT

West Rd.

DORSET

Lower Hollow Rd.

to MANCHESTER CENTER

Church St.

New York

Fishing Vermont's Streams and Lakes
© 1992 Backcountry Publications

towns surrounding Manchester Center are doubly blessed to be home to both the Mettawee and the Batten Kill, two of the state's premier trout streams.

The river begins up on Dorset Mountain in the town of Dorset as a tiny brook which is fed by several other small trickles of streams until they all meet where Lower Hollow Road crosses the river for the third time. This is extremely small water, although it will hold some good native brook trout for those willing to scramble up the mountain during the early weeks of the trout season each year. The river bed is overgrown with tree limbs and shrubs, making casting difficult. This is the case throughout much of the seventeen-mile run this river takes.

Access to most of the run of the Mettawee is had by following VT 30 out of Manchester Center, through Dorset, the northeastern corner of Rupert, and on into Pawlet. At the village of East Rupert the Mettawee converges with several small brooks, right near the intersection of VT 30 and VT 315. VT 315 follows the flow of a small tributary which heads down to the main stem just to the north of East Rupert. This is not a large brook by any means. For that matter, the main stem of the river is still extremely small. As you follow it, however, you will begin to see why the Mettawee is considered a classic trout stream.

While this river is narrow and shallow, it also runs through rural settings that receive little or no fishing pressure. The Mettawee simply does not look as though it held big trout. But hidden behind the tree lines and farm fields are countless bends and tiny brook tributaries which all hold decent-sized holes of surprising depths. The holes in turn are the homes for a thriving trout population.

If you drive north on VT 30 until you reach Dorset village, you will find that Church Street heads west out of the village for a short distance before it intersects with West Road. West Road is your key to successful fishing on this part of the Mettawee. To the southwest is Bear Mountain. To the northwest all the Pawlet Valley and the Mettawee spread out before you. The intersection of Church Street and West Road actually marks the beginnings of another set of small brooks which will meet the main stem downstream in East Rupert. This area can be very productive in the spring, and anglers will want to check it out thoroughly during April and May. Use your lightest fly gear or your smallest ultralight rig, though. These are small fish, mostly rainbows and brookies.

This whole upper portion of the Mettawee comes to an end as you leave East Rupert and head north. From here VT 30 will lead you along the eastern shoreline of the river until you get a mile past North Rupert. The Mettawee is still a small piece of water here. You will find that the surface of the water is usually quite smooth, although the river is not always slow-moving. The Mettawee is also narrow, about shin deep in most sections throughout this area.

Still, the fishing is good. While there may not be much water in the river, the water running through here is ice cold. Brook trout find this especially pleasing, and you will find them in good numbers. You will also start to see more and more rainbow trout as well as some browns.

As you head north out of North Rupert and into Pawlet, you will arrive at perhaps the best part of the river. The river bank is heavily overgrown, which makes fly-fishing extremely tough. I fished in here one midsummer day with Wes Carkin, the guide who helped in the preparation of the chapter on the Batten Kill River. Wes brought his favorite custom rod and I my favorite Fenwick HMS graphite. We both started out by using identical number-2 Panther Martins, throwing alternating casts into the narrow little stream.

I managed to catch a tree branch every fourth or fifth cast, while Wes kept his line effortlessly free of entanglements. If you think this became irritating, you're right. But far more embarrassing was how much more successful Wes was than I in getting strikes and fish. He caught and released two fish to every one I pulled in. Since Wes was the guide on this fishing trip, however, I should have expected that, and it made somewhat less of a difference when I realized just how many strikes we were getting, even though the air temperature was a hazy 85 degrees.

The water was quite low, as Vermont was suffering the effects of a serious drought. The southern third of the state had not seen a good rainstorm in well over six weeks, and water levels on the Mettawee were down more than two feet below normal. Still, the water temperature was under 65 degrees, and much of the stream was hidden in the shade of the many tree branches. While we were unable to get them to strike the way their smaller compatriots did, we spotted several very large brown trout lurking in the shadows.

Wes pointed out that the whole portion of the Mettawee that runs from the Rupert/Pawlet line through the confluence with Flower Brook in Pawlet village was like this. Indeed, this six-mile piece of river is teeming with trout in the 6- to 16-inch range, hidden in the holes and well-shaded little riffles that one finds mixed in the knee-deep water. Several bridges cross the river in this area, and all of them are likely spots to begin your fishing trip.

Early in the season caddis fly hatches are the most common. However, as temperatures heat up in May and June, Hendricksons, stoneflies, and various beautifully colored Cahills will appear on the water. I especially love the Cream-Colored Cahills, which appear to be so dainty when they light on the water's surface. Fortunately the trout seem to share my affection for these lovely insects, and you will see fish feeding voraciously on them during the late afternoon hours during June and July.

Perhaps the most dramatic, if not the most beautiful times in the spring trout season are those first days when the large insect hatches begin to occur on the stream. Now some of you may have a natural aversion to this phenomenon. After all, you say, don't these lovely little hatches act as prelude to black fly season? You remember black flies? It has been said they can carry off a fully outfitted trout angler while in midcast. But the early fly hatches are quite beautiful, if only you know what to look for.

First of all remember that flies are trout food and that a trout with a plentiful food supply is more apt than not to rise to the surface after emerging flies. The sight of the first rainbow clearing the water at the top of a rapid is one of the most exciting things you can observe on the stream. Similarly, there is a kind of grace to the way a big brown trout will create a swirl on the slowly moving water at the bottom of a run as it chases after nymphs attempting to rise to the surface. And do not forget the way the native brookie slaps in its sideways attack at the flies on the surface slick. Watching for sights like these is half the reason for being out on the water in the first place.

But there is something fairly spectacular about the flies themselves. The most common of the species we have here is the caddis. They spend most of their lives underwater, attached to the bottoms of rocks. When they emerge, they do so in large numbers, sitting in the slick of the water's surface until their wings dry off and they can fly away. Then they all move together upstream in a huge swirling column until they rest to lay their eggs and die. The stonefly lives underwater most of the time too, but when it emerges, it crawls out onto a flat rock. The

The Mettawee offers anglers some great opportunities for big trout, but casting can be tight in places like this.

stonefly looks rather like some type of mutant life form from another planet when it is in this stage. It adheres itself to the rock and lets its skin dry out. Then it splits out of this shell-like container and emerges as a winged fly. It will fly off to a tree branch to seek out a mate and will lay its eggs back in the water before it too expires.

The mayflies are like the caddis in that they will attempt to dry off their wings in the water, but soon after they have done so, they will fly up and down over the water's surface with a spinning action. This graceful motion is perhaps my favorite among all the behavior which aquatic insects exhibit, and mayflies spinning in large numbers are a very dramatic sight.

I have only discussed three of the major species of insects you're apt to see on the stream, but rest assured there are many more, and each holds the rapt attention of all trout life. Therefore you should probably spend some time on the water every now and then just looking at what the flies are doing. You can be sure that when the insects are active the fish that feed on them will be as well.

Back on the Mettawee, you will see an increasing number of large insect hatches as you move downstream from Pawlet village and into the area where the river finally begins to open up and widen near Butternut Bend. There are an increasing number of riffles, runs, and deep pools here as VT 30 continues to follow the river on its eastern shore. The river winds through some very pastoral settings, beautiful farmland and fields. I have been warned that it is a good policy to check with landowners before wading through the river on their property, even if you do not plan on using their land as access. Vermont law stipulates that no landowner may actually own a river that runs through his property, but many Pawlet farmers have had tough times with hunters and hikers and wish to keep their privacy. It is far better to quickly ask permission first than to engage in an endless and heated argument over the fine points of the law later, when you are already out on the stream.

As you reach Butternut Bend, you will come across Butternut Bend Falls, a beautiful place which is the only natural obstruction to the river in Vermont. The fishing both up and downstream from the falls is excellent, but you will run into two paradoxical obstacles here. The first is the fact that many folks in this area know about the falls and make it a swimming hole during the heat of summer. The second problem is that the land around the falls is all posted. If you hike in from downstream, though, you should be able to fish much of the productive water without incident.

At Butternut Bend a small back road enters from the west and follows the river through the 1½-mile stretch before you come upon VT 153. VT 153 heads north and in a little less than 2 miles it meets VT 30. This little dogleg of the Mettawee is filled with some of the prettiest trout water you will see in this seventeen-mile run. There are lots of little twists and turns which hold good-sized brown trout and rainbows. In fact, the rainbow fishing here can be extremely good, especially during May and June.

As you head north on VT 30 again, you will come across Button Falls Road on the west side of the highway, just before VT 30 intersects with VT 149 at Blossoms Corners. Both Button Falls Road and VT 149 offer access to the Mettawee during the last 1–1½ miles that it winds through northern Pawlet and into New York State. Midway between the VT

30/149 junction and the New York line, Wells Brook feeds into the river, a very worthwhile place to explore. During the fall, large brown trout head up Wells Brook and into Mill Brook.

Mill Brook is the northern fork of this little two-part tributary and is fed by Little Pond in the town of Wells. For its part, Little Pond is really the bottom spur of Lake St. Catherine, a fabulous lake trout and rainbow location. Little Pond is best known, though, for its large-mouth bass and northern pike. If you happen to be fishing along this most northwestern stretch of the Mettawee, bring along a canoe and try these two fabulous pieces of flat water while you are at it.

6

The Ottauquechee River

This well-known river winds its way through the towns of Sherburne, Bridgewater, Woodstock, Hartford, and Hartland before emptying into the Connecticut River near North Hartland village. It is not anywhere near as large a tributary to the Connecticut as its neighbor the White River; however, it holds the same abundant variety of game fish.

The Ottauquechee begins at the confluence of two very small brooks near Kent Pond in Sherburne. The outflow of the pond also feeds into the river, and it is here that you will first find small brook trout. The whole section of the river that runs through Sherburne Center, along US 4, and into West Bridgewater is quite small. Much of the river is reached by walking through the many fields near the road. Many of these fields are protected by electric fence, and anglers will want to ask permission of the landowners before crossing over to the river banks.

While most of the fish you will catch in this stretch of water are brook trout, you will also find some rainbows and browns, particularly during their respective spring and fall spawning runs. There is plenty of good cover for fish to hide in. Tree branches make some beautiful overhangs, and there are lots of boulders in the river, creating good holes where fish hold. Wading is easy, and fly-anglers will do well here.

The stretch from Sherburne Center downstream to West Bridgewater is some of the most pristine water you will find on the Ottauquechee and strangely enough, also some of the most easily accessible. US 4 runs

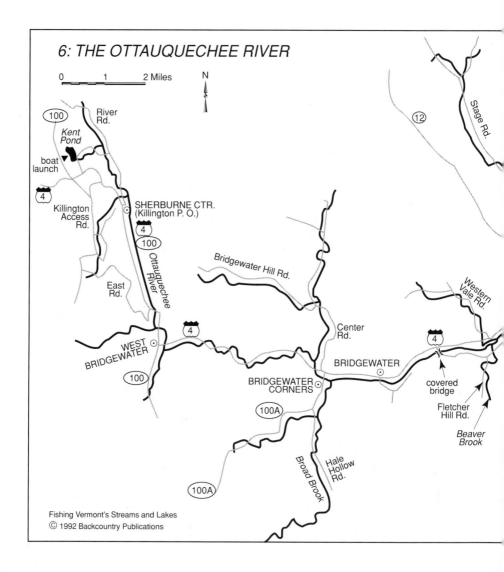

6: THE OTTAUQUECHEE RIVER

0   1   2 Miles   N

100   River Rd.

Kent Pond

boat launch

4   Killington Access Rd.

SHERBURNE CTR. (Killington P. O.)

4

100

Bridgewater Hill Rd.

Ottauquechee River

East Rd.

4

Center Rd.

WEST BRIDGEWATER

100

BRIDGEWATER CORNERS

100A

BRIDGEWATER

Western Vale Rd.

4   covered bridge

Fletcher Hill Rd.

Beaver Brook

Broad Brook

Hale Hollow Rd.

100A

12

Stage Rd.

Fishing Vermont's Streams and Lakes
© 1992 Backcountry Publications

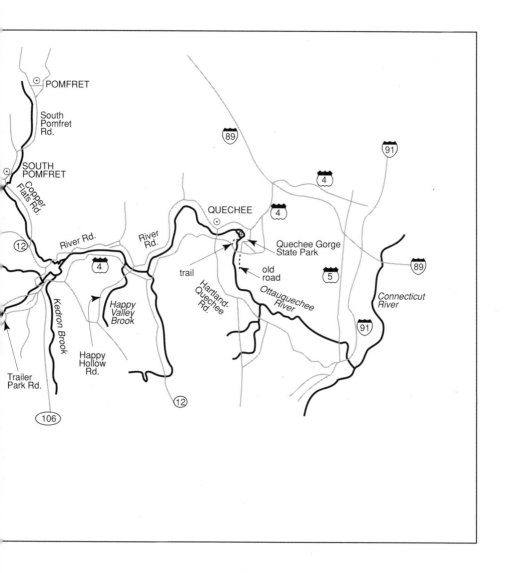

along the western bank of the river as it runs south, providing you with plenty of good places to pull over and start fishing. There are several good spots to get out and hike through the water in search of the many native brook trout and wild rainbows. Let me describe three of them for you.

While US 4 only crosses the river twice in this 4½-mile stretch, there are many logical places to make such a crossing yourself. The first, as you start from the upstream side, just south of Sherburne Center, is a small dead-end road about a half-mile out of the village. I would not park on this road or next to the bridge that takes it over the river, but park off US 4 and walk in instead. This makes your vehicle much less of an impediment to traffic. From here you can wade all the way back to the village with ease.

Another good area to fish and wade is where Mission Farm Road enters US 4 after crossing the river, about a 1½ miles from West Bridgewater. The road runs parallel to US 4 and offers anglers easy access to the other side of the river. A third alternative is to enter the river where Falls Brook runs into the river near West Bridgewater. There are literally dozens of good places to get into the river along this section, so it almost doesn't matter where you start.

As you cross the Bridgewater town line, the fishing continues to be for rainbows and brookies. Again, the water is very clear and clean, which makes it ideal for those of you who like to dry-fly-fish. I love this kind of fishing, and I enjoy water like this in particular. The river is still fairly small, although as you get toward Bridgewater Corners, the North Branch feeds in, and things begin to open up a bit after that. Attractor patterns like the Royal Coachman work extremely well throughout this region, and you can make use of your very lightest fly gear too. I would not want to use anything much larger or heavier than a 7½-foot rod, at 4-weight.

As the Ottauquechee widens slightly, you run into some of the river's brown trout. I have not mentioned this particular species much yet, because you are not apt to catch them with any regularity until you get into the middle section of the river. That is not to say browns are absent, though. In 1989 the state Fish and Wildlife Department performed an electroshock population survey of the Ottauquechee and found that it supports large numbers of brown trout throughout its run. Forty percent of the estimated populations of brown, rainbow,

A bridge spans the beautiful Quechee Gorge.

and brook trout were determined to be at least a year old. While brook trout made up 44.3 percent of the estimated population and were therefore the largest group, brown trout weighed in at 39 percent. Rainbows accounted for 16.7 percent.

Another interesting finding of this 1989 population study is that while there are fewer rainbow trout in the Ottauquechee than there are members of the other two species, rainbows are more apt to be yearlings or older. Over 59 percent of all the rainbows counted were at least a year old, as compared to 43 percent for browns and 30 percent for brook trout. However, this result may be only a chance finding, for out of the year-old or better trout counted in the survey, only 25 percent were rainbows. Brown trout made up 42 percent of this group and brookies 34 percent. What the study unmistakably shows is that the Ottauquechee has a superb population of brown trout. Rainbows are surviving, though they are not doing as well. In fact the study indicates that rainbows may not be present in the very upper reaches of the river to any great degree, while browns and brookies are. The study did not differentiate between wild and stocked fish, however.

But we should get back to the river while we are discussing the trout population and see what happens as you move downstream from West Bridgewater and through the rest of that part of the Ottauquechee which follows US 4 east toward Woodstock. The highway crosses the river six times between West Bridgewater and Bridgewater village. All these spots are ideal places to begin a fishing trip, and the segment that runs through the northern edge of the Ottauquechee Wildlife Management Area, just a mile to the west of Bridgewater Corners, is particularly good. Here you will find rainbows and browns mixed in with brook trout.

I suggest you check the mouths of Broad Brook and the North Branch. Broad Brook runs alongside VT 100A from its mouth up to the intersection with Pinney Hollow Brook. Thereafter your best bet for keeping on Broad Brook is to turn off VT 100A and onto Hale Hollow Road. The North Branch is best approached via Center Road, off US 4 and then Chateauguay Road. Some folks in the area actually refer to this stream as Chateauguay Brook. Regardless of what you call it, both this piece of water and Broad Brook are excellent places to fish for brookies and rainbows. The water gets a bit deeper as you go downstream from Bridgewater Corners, particularly as you pass behind the Bridgewater Mill Mall. As on much of the upper Ottauquechee, dry flies work well. Patterns like Elk Hair Caddis and Adams work best.

As you head out of Bridgewater and into Woodstock, you will find that the river is open and the water is exposed to sunlight during much of the day. The six-mile stretch from Bridgewater village to about a mile west of Woodstock village is quite shallow too. Access along US 4 is good, perhaps a little too good. This area receives significant fishing pressure and really is not up to it. There are numerous brooks which feed into the river and a few good, deep holes. These places can be productive, and you will find a good mix of browns and rainbows in isolated spots.

Once you get past this area, you will be into a beautiful length of river which mixes pools and riffles with some very exciting brown trout fishing. As you head downstream from near West Woodstock, another small brook enters the river, and from here through Woodstock village, the fishing really picks up. The only drawback is that you'll find a good number of sunbathers and other anglers in this area. Access is easy off US 4, and there is a considerable amount of traffic. You would do best to fish here at first light or after the sun has gone down for the day to avoid the crowds.

In the center of the village VT 12 intersects with US 4. While you can continue to follow the river via US 4, you can also get access from the north side of the stream by taking VT 12 until it intersects with River Road. This back road will take you out of Woodstock and into Hartford following the river's shoreline. In fact you can wind your way all the way to the Quechee Gorge State Park on back roads.

Two interesting things happen to the Ottauquechee in this section. As you leave Woodstock village and get about a mile out of town, the river widens. This supplies you with a greater number of places to fish for big browns and rainbows. On the other hand, you are now also going to come up against the four hydroelectric dams on the Ottauquechee.

The first dam you will encounter is located in Taftsville, which is a small village right on the Woodstock/Hartford town line. The tailwater fishing here is good, although it should be noted that this dam has recently been designated a "run of the river" site. This means that the dam will only be producing power when the natural flow of the

Ottauquechee allows it; it will no longer hold back water for this purpose. Access for fishing at the first dam is not good, unfortunately.

Below Taftsville, in the village of Quechee, you will find the second dam. This hydro site offers some good tailwater fishing as well, although the water immediately upstream is slow, silty, and fairly unproductive. This is an interesting place in that below it you will find the Deweys Mills Pond, which is formed by the third dam on the river. The pond is a viable warm-water fishery and holds a decent large-mouth bass population. Anglers can do very well here by working along the Deweys Mills dam with crankbaits, jigs, and spinnerbaits.

Below the Deweys Mills dam, you come to perhaps the most dramatic feature of the Ottauquechee River, the Quechee Gorge. The gorge runs for a mile and offers some of the deepest holes and pools in the river. It is also the most difficult stretch to get to, and wading is extremely hazardous. Don't forget, there is a dam upstream which regulates the flow of the river. Because of fluctuating water levels and poor footing, this is not an area to trifle with unless you know what you are doing.

Marty Banak runs the Vermont Fly Fishing School at the Quechee Inn at Marshland Farm. He guides this difficult section of the Ottauquechee as well as the lower White River and is much experienced in working up and down the treacherous shoreline of the gorge. Access to the river in the gorge is possible by foot. On the east side of the gorge there is an old road (closed to cars) which slopes steadily toward the southern or downstream end. There is a path on the west shore which takes anglers to the upstream end. These paths are well marked and are an easy hike down to the river. As a point of reference the bridge where US 4 crosses the gorge bisects this stretch of river exactly in half.

Fishing the east shore has the advantage of taking the angler into the area where the gorge ends and access steadily begins to improve. Here, as is the case throughout the gorge, you will be casting to some huge brown trout as well as some very large rainbows. If you fish this portion of the gorge, you can work with caddis, Hendricksons, and March Browns. Stoneflies work well throughout the gorge, while anglers working the upstream area might want to stick with heavily weighted Woolly Buggers and a weighted sinking-tip line. Use a heavy rod in here; not only are the fish quite large, but you will also want the extra power of a big rod to deliver your fly to the river while you're standing on some fairly high rock formations.

Access to the river from below the gorge is best effected via the Hartland Quechee Road, which runs south out of Quechee village— not that this is going to do you much good, however. Unfortunately, the 4- or 5-mile stretch of river from just below the gorge all the way down to the North Hartland Dam is a waste of time for the serious angler. The water is flat, warm, and almost completely devoid of game fish. There are a few largemouth bass, some perch, and large numbers of bullhead at the upper end, but little else in terms of wild fish. The Fish and Wildlife Department has stocked this area with rainbow trout, but they do not seem to be surviving well, making this a "put and take" fishery of sorts. You would do far better to ignore the area upstream from the dam and concentrate instead on the water below it and downstream into the Connecticut River. This 1½-mile area holds some good rainbow trout and some smallmouth bass.

One final note on the Ottauquechee River. Most of the insect hatches like the caddis, mayfly, stonefly, and the hellgrammite or Dobsonfly near the river's mouth take place just about two weeks earlier than they do on the White River's mouth, which is just a bit to the north in Hartford. This means you can start fishing on the Ottauquechee at the very beginning of Vermont's trout season and use your experience with the various hatches on the White later on.

Section Two

Central Vermont

7

The White River

I've fished the White River quite a bit over the years, paying particular attention to the headwaters up in the Patterson Brook area in the town of Granville. But in the summer months I like to spend time just downstream from where the White tumbles down that steep mountainside up in the northern part of Granville and fish it to the south, near Lower Granville and Hancock.

I buy my winter wood in the spring or summer, depending on how early I get ambitious in any given year. These trips to and from my home and the big wood pile I buy from bring me past the Granville Bowl Mill, an interesting place where they make and wholesale wooden bowls. The White River runs past here, right downstream from where the Clark and Patterson brooks merge with the headwaters to this classic trout stream.

The mile or so just downstream from the Granville Bowl Mill is particularly good fishing for small brook trout and rainbows, and the water for the next two miles after that point is equally productive. This is very different water from the White River many of us know. In Bethel the White is a wide, deep, and fast-flowing torrent. But up in Granville it's a fairly small, clear-running stream which features some of the prettiest runs and riffles I've seen anywhere in the state of Vermont.

I like to wade in to the south of the bowl mill and often find some big surprises in this small piece of water. For openers, the water temperature is a chilly 55 degrees, making the fish very active, even during the relative heat of the 75- to 80-degree days I choose to go fishing in July and early August. I usually can catch and release six rainbows or brookies using number-12 Yellow Humpies and number-14 Grasshoppers in a little over an hour, and I'll sometimes lose up to another dozen fish as well. All these trout strike hard and fight bravely, making for a very enjoyable break from my wood hauling.

This piece of the White River is a fly-angler's delight. It features one small, 4- to 6-foot deep run after another, each one appearing almost more gorgeous than the one before. I have found that I will be standing on one small run, casting blissfully at the rising trout and promising that this would be the very last one I would venture upstream for, only to see the next run up ahead looking even more beautiful and fertile than the one I was enjoying. Just when I think I have had enough, a new stretch of water beckons. I cannot resist, and I don't think many other anglers would be able to leave the stream at all under these circumstances.

This is how the White begins. The main stem runs a length of fifty-seven miles from Granville to its mouth at the Connecticut River in the town of White River Junction. For quite a long way over its upper reaches, through Granville, Hancock, and Rochester, the river is narrow as it winds through farm fields, woods, and along VT 100. It widens out somewhat as it passes through the southern part of Rochester and moves through Stockbridge, which is where the upper White River ends and the middle river picks up. The middle runs through the central portions of Stockbridge along VT 107, through a corner of Bethel and into Royalton where it runs into VT 14. The lower river continues out of Royalton, through Sharon, Hartford, and out into the Connecticut River.

The state Fish and Wildlife Department has performed some creel surveys to determine how anglers are doing when they fish the river and have discovered some interesting things about the White River's fish and those of us who pursue them. Studies were made in 1965, 1971, and 1986. In 1965 and 1986, surveyors worked the 32.7-mile length of the river from Rochester to Hartford. In 1971, though, they concentrated only on the segment between Stockbridge and Bethel.

What they discovered was that 71 percent of all of the fish reported to have been caught were rainbow trout. Brown trout made up 20 percent of the survey, while brook trout figured in for only 5 percent.

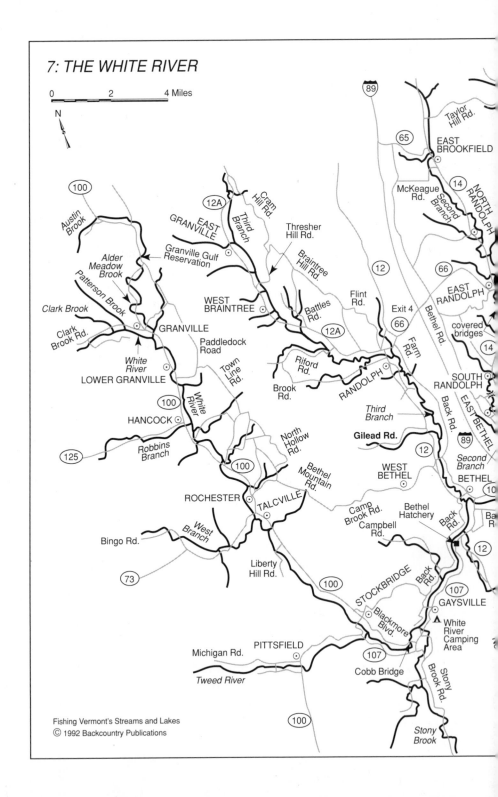

7: THE WHITE RIVER

0   2   4 Miles

N

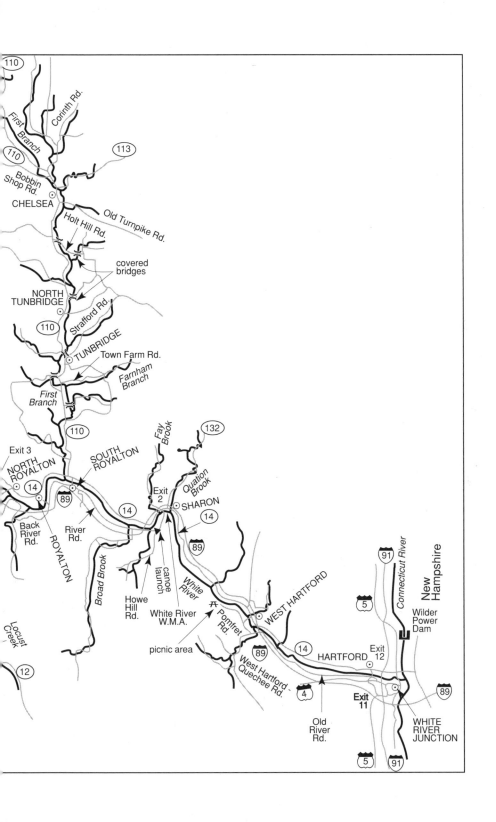

Four percent of the fish creeled were smallmouth bass. Interestingly enough, 53 percent of the rainbows were stocked fish, as were 58 percent of the brown trout. This is significant, as it shows that the White River holds a good-sized wild trout population.

Another interesting set of figures showed that anglers fishing the Stockbridge-to-Bethel section of the river caught and released 168 juvenile Atlantic salmon in 1986. Fish and Wildlife stocked 125,000 salmon parr in the middle part of the river in 1985, so this is not a terribly surprising development.

Trout stocked in the White River during the survey years were as follows: 8,000 rainbows and 7,000 browns were stocked in 1965; 4,000 rainbows and 6,400 browns in 1971; and 7,200 rainbows and 8,000 browns in 1986.

The information that the creel survey gathered about the kinds of people who fish on the White River was at least as interesting as what was learned about the trout. Twenty-seven percent of all the anglers who frequented the river between 1965 and 1986 used fly gear. They tended, like most of the bait- and lure-anglers, to fish in the middle portion of the river, although they were also well represented in the upper river. Most of the fly-anglers—60 percent of this group, in fact— came from outside Vermont to fish. According to the conclusions of the study, which was submitted in 1987, the White River remains a high-priority fishery for the state Fish and Wildlife Department. Plans were made in 1987 to stock 10,000 trout per year in the main stem of the river during the months of May and June. The need for these trout is vital, notwithstanding the fact that roughly half of all the trout reported to have been caught in 1986 were wild.

The upper White River is my favorite stretch. It is the best for anglers who prefer to fly-fish and do not mind working in close proximity to overhanging trees and tree-root-bordered shorelines. It is also the most beautiful, as it flows through the least populated townships of its run. During the early spring, this is the best part of the river, as it runs clearer than the portions downstream from Rochester. When the snowmelt leaves the lower two-thirds of the White River high and silty, I can usually find some good trout in Granville and Hancock.

The river is crossed by VT 100 at six points between Granville and Rochester. All these locations are logical places to begin a search for productive trout water. However, you should not limit your wanderings to the bridge crossings. VT 100 follows the river closely, and there are plenty of other good places to pull over and wade in.

This whole stretch of the river through these three little towns is great water to work either from the shore or by wading. The depths do vary, especially at the river's many turns, but for the most part, the stream is knee deep, allowing you excellent access whether you prefer to wear hip or chest waders. This section is especially exciting during the spring and fall spawning seasons. I take a lot of my clients to this part of the White River during the months of May and September. In the spring the rainbows tear up through the upper river to nest and lay eggs. It is a beautiful sight to watch these fish pair off and move along the rapids together. Fishing for them can be a little tough, though, as they are usually much more interested in finding mates than in feeding.

However, the fall run is quite a different story. Brookies and brown trout always appear to be much more aggressive than rainbows are

The Vermont Fish and Wildlife Department repeatedly stocks the length of the White River with trout and Atlantic salmon. Anglers are warned not to keep salmon and there is a $500 fine for violations of this law.

during their respective spawning runs. I find that I am always able to locate active brook trout in Granville by wading in from one of the places where VT 100 crosses and heading slowly upstream. The trick is to take a little more time than normal when casting to each of the small pools here. The trout are engaged in their nesting ritual and will not spook very easily, and for the same reason, they may tend to ignore your fly or lure for quite a while.

I took two clients from western Massachusetts fishing the entire run from just south of Rochester village all the way north into Granville one September day. We found lots of active browns and even a few rainbows throughout Rochester and into Hancock. These fish were very aggressive and hit our lines almost the instant we began to retrieve. In the fall streamers like the Black and Gray Ghost seem to work the best, although you can also do very well with Montana nymphs. You do not have to fish all that deep through Rochester and into the southern half of the Hancock stretch, maybe only six inches to a foot below the surface. However, as the three of us moved up into the northern half of the river in Hancock, conditions slowly began to change. The river got a little narrower and shallower, forcing us to pick our way through patches of shin-deep water to get to the deeper pools holding fish.

We also found that we had to switch from our streamers and nymphs to deeper-swimming flies like weighted Woolly Buggers. My clients switched over to ultralight spinning gear and fluorescent painted Panther Martins. I argued that the brightly colored spinners were far more appropriate to smallmouth or pike fishing but was pleasantly surprised to find that both these gentlemen caught very nice sized trout on them nonetheless. The brook trout were found in large concentrations at the mouths of the many small brooks and springs which feed the river when it is at this small stage.

During the late spring and early summer months, I like to head farther downstream and fish the middle part of the White. As the West Branch enters the White at the intersection of VT 73 and VT 100, the river begins to widen, and the whole complexion of the stream changes. It twists and turns through a small section of Pittsfield and on into Stockbridge, where the Tweed River (also noted for its trout fishing) enters, before heading sharply to the east near the intersection of VT 100 and VT 107. It was in this area, right near Cobb Bridge, that a returning Atlantic salmon was spotted in 1986. The sighting was very significant, as this fish was the first returning salmon found this far up the White River since George Washington was president of the United States.

There are not a lot of good places to pull your car off the road in this area, but if you are willing to do a little walking along the highways and in the river itself, you will find what you need. This is a very productive stretch for rainbow trout, and you will find them spread out all along the rapids and faster-moving runs which mark this piece of the stream. The river has opened up a bit too, which means that you will find less tree cover and shade for the fish to hide under. Consequently, you will have to concentrate your efforts on the wakes of the growing number of large rocks and boulders which poke out from the surface of the water.

As the river flows into the village of Gaysville, you see the White River Valley Camping Area. This area is heavily fished, and you will have to look hard for places to call your own during the height of the summer season. Still, the river does occasionally bend a little way away from VT 107, offering you opportunities to get some breathing space. A bridge that crosses the river at Gaysville is where most anglers start their forays. You may prefer to pull over a half-mile either up or downstream from this point instead.

The one good thing about the bridge near the campground is that it gives you access to a small road which runs parallel to VT 107, on the opposite side of the river. This is the Back Road to Gaysville, it is not all that well traveled, and it offers you some good places to get out and fish. The Back Road extends all the way up to VT 12, where you will want to turn south toward Bethel. VT 12 meets VT 107 shortly thereafter and continues to run along the northern shoreline of the White River.

The short section of the White River which runs alongside VT 107 from Bethel to North Royalton is noteworthy as it bridges two major tributaries. The Third Branch enters just south of Bethel and is one of the most exciting pieces of trout water I know. It flows from East Granville, through Braintree, and on into Randolph before heading to Bethel. The fishing for big brown trout is excellent from the mouth of the Third Branch all the way upstream, past Bethel village. The tributary is very wide and deep, so anglers will want to take care when they wade it.

A typical view of the middle White River.

The Second Branch runs along VT 14 from southern Williamstown, through Brookfield, Randolph, and a small corner of Bethel before meeting the main stem in Royalton. This branch runs through a lightly populated area for quite some time as you work it from the mouth upstream, offering you some great rainbow and brown trout fishing. There are two beautiful covered bridges which cross the river in South and East Randolph too. VT 14 also heads south from VT 107, following the main stem of the White River to its next major tributary.

The First Branch of the White River enters the main stem in Royalton too, right where VT 110 meets VT 14. This tributary runs from the southern edge of Washington into Chelsea, Tunbridge, and back into Royalton. There are six covered bridges along its route, and each of them provides great access to this stream. Dozens of small brooks feed the First Branch throughout its run, providing fabulous brook trout fishing. There are lots of deep holes in this stream that hold browns and rainbows. However, summer water temperatures on the first branch can be murderously high, making fishing awfully tough.

As the main stem of the river flows from Royalton into Sharon, it slows down somewhat, offering canoeists some fine opportunities. Perhaps one of the most pleasant runs to canoe starts in Sharon where Fay Brook Road crosses the river and meets Howe Hill Road, just to the west of Sharon village and Exit 2 on I-89. The river is slow, as I mentioned, but it is also very deep, and the fishing for big browns and rainbows is excellent. You will pass the White River Wildlife Management Area on the southern shore, right where the river bends sharply southward. There is an island in the middle of the river here, and the fishing along its edge and just downstream can be very good. The canoe run will continue for about four miles to the picnic area right on the Sharon/Pomfret town line.

The best flies to use here are big weighted stonefly nymphs. You will also want to bring along a second fly rod set up with sink-tip line. I would advise you use the larger of your fly rods, say a 7- or 8-weight rig with a good, long leader with no less that a 4X tippet. Since streamers and muddlers work well in this area too, you will want an extralong rod to give those big, heavy flies a little extra push when you cast them.

The access from VT 14 in this stretch varies somewhat. There are lots of rockledges which prevent easy access, but these ledges are also accompanied by deep holes which hold some of the biggest trout in the whole river. There are big caddis hatches here during the spring, and the long, slow-moving glides are perfect for floating mayflies during June and July. While the stoneflies will work way down deep almost all season long, you can use smaller emerging stonefly imitations during July and early August. You will see some of the best stonefly hatches at dusk during the late summer.

The water from West Hartford along the seven miles to the bridge in Hartford village is quite flat. Once you get into Hartford village, though, you will find more and more shallow water in between all those nice holes where the big trout lie hiding. You will also find smallmouth bass mixed in the pools and riffles. The best fast water will run along the rock ledges. While the river here could be fished by canoe, it is tough to do so in the middle of the summer. The river dries up considerably then.

From the village the river has an almost uniform bottom and is not all that deep. There are some big trout as you head into White River

Junction, but they are not plentiful. The river is very wide now, and your best bet is the fishing for smallmouth, which can be extremely good through White River Junction and into the Connecticut River. There are some large rainbows to be caught right at the mouth, too, as well as some huge smallmouth bass.

Two important points should be discussed as we close out this chapter, both regarding the White River's mouth. The first is that anglers should watch out for Atlantic salmon. I have already mentioned that these fish are stocked in the river, but I have not mentioned that they are protected by law. In fact there is a $500 fine for violating this regulation. If you do catch a salmon, all you have to do is release it back into the water and there is no harm done. Atlantic salmon parr do resemble brown trout, however. The biggest difference is that while brown trout have rounded tails, the salmon's tail is forked and pointed. Also, the salmon is a solid-colored fish, while the similarly tinged brown trout has brown and orange spots on its body.

Finally, as you fish the mouth of the White where it enters the Connecticut, BE CAREFUL OF RISING WATER LEVELS. Just four miles upstream from the White's mouth lies the Wilder power dam. The water can rise eighteen inches in just fifteen minutes when the turbines are in operation, causing you to have to scramble for shore to avoid being swept downstream.

8

Ripton Gorge and
The Middlebury River

The South Branch of the Middlebury River is a small piece of water which begins in the mountains just to the west of the top of Middlebury Gap. The Middlebury follows VT 125 to the west and empties into Otter Creek just to the south of the main village of Middlebury. The source of the South Branch is tiny Pleiad Lake, right at the Middlebury College Snow Bowl, a ski area where the college's internationally famous ski team practices. In fact this beautiful lake is accessible via the nearby Long Trail.

As you follow VT 125 westward from the Snow Bowl and into the village of Ripton, the Middle Branch of the Middlebury joins the flow, and the small stream grows a little bit wider. However, even when the North Branch joins the main flow a few miles on, this river is still a very small mountain stream. Situated roughly two thousand feet above sea level, the river remains cold all summer long, offering anglers some fantastic opportunities after most central Vermont rivers have turned too warm to fish during July and August.

Although the Middlebury River is a very small stream, about the width of many of the state's medium-sized brooks, it is complex, amounting to three distinct trout streams all wrapped up into one. The upper and lower parts of the river are separated by a two-mile gorge located near the village of Ripton. These two upper and lower stretches

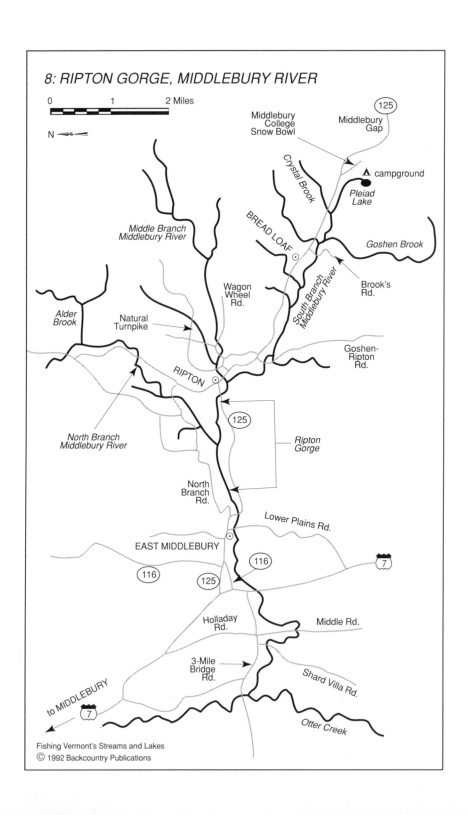

8: RIPTON GORGE, MIDDLEBURY RIVER

0   1   2 Miles

N

Middlebury College Snow Bowl

Middlebury Gap

125

▲ campground

Crystal Brook

Pleiad Lake

BREAD LOAF

Middle Branch Middlebury River

Goshen Brook

Wagon Wheel Rd.

South Branch Middlebury River

Brook's Rd.

Alder Brook

Natural Turnpike

Goshen-Ripton Rd.

RIPTON

125

North Branch Middlebury River

Ripton Gorge

North Branch Rd.

Lower Plains Rd.

EAST MIDDLEBURY

116

116

7

125

Holladay Rd.

Middle Rd.

3-Mile Bridge Rd.

Shard Villa Rd.

to MIDDLEBURY

7

Otter Creek

Fishing Vermont's Streams and Lakes
© 1992 Backcountry Publications

are great water for native brookies and wild rainbows. There are numerous pull-overs where anglers can park their cars, get into their gear, and hike down into the river. Fly-anglers will love these two areas, as there are few overhangs to disrupt a long, double-haul cast. Spin-anglers will enjoy the occasional deep pools and runs which hold a few lunker-size brown trout.

I have a preference for the upper part of the river, just before it heads into Ripton Gorge (sometimes also referred to as Middlebury Gorge). This is a small piece of water which is reached by the few pull-overs you will find along VT 125. The banks are steep and go down for quite a distance, which keeps a lot of anglers out of this area. But the fishing for browns, brookies, and rainbows is very good, and I like to fish it with a small fly rod and an assortment of mayflies, stoneflies, and terrestrials. Perhaps the most effective fly to use here is a large Humpy, since it is easy to watch as it cascades through the fast-moving current.

The lower part of the river as it winds through Middlebury township is lovely, too, and is a small piece of water with lots of holes for trout to hide in. Like the rest of the river, this is classic pocket water. There are some deep holes in this area where you can use heavy nymphs and streamers too. Woolly Buggers, Muddler Minnows, and Maribou Muddlers are among my favorites.

Best times to fish these two pieces of the Middlebury River are first thing in the morning and late in the afternoon. This means it is the perfect stream for the nine-to-fiver. Grab an hour or two before work, and then hit it again when you get out for the day.

But then there is the gorge. The Ripton Gorge, as it is best known, is one of the best and worst pieces of trout water I've ever fished. The best because it lies more than 150 vertical feet below VT 125 and holds the cold temperatures of dawn throughout the day. The best also because the pools can run over 6-feet deep and will hold trout well into the 12- to 18-inch range. And once again the best because very few anglers venture into the gorge to fish the river there.

But Ripton Gorge has the defects of its virtues. Just because it lies over 150 feet below the highway, access is extremely difficult. The hike down to the river is extremely steep, and the footing sometimes quite dangerous. Similarly, once you are at the bottom of the gorge, the footing through and around the river bed is very treacherous. Often an angler will be forced to climb up along sheer rock ledges of over 30 feet, just to move up a few yards along the stream. Also, you may end up following one bank for just a few pools too far, only to find you must backtrack 100 yards or more to find a safe point to wade across the river.

Approximately at the point where North Branch Road meets the highway (just to the east of East Middlebury village) you will find a small concrete bridge where VT 125 spans the stream. The climb down to the river can be tricky, but this is the easiest access to the downstream end of Ripton Gorge. As I pointed out, you can choose to enter the gorge from further upstream where you will find some extremely tough footing. For the first-time visitor, I would strongly recommend starting at the bridge. The hike will begin pleasantly enough from the bridge and there are not all that many obstacles for you to worry about until you have ventured a quarter- to a half-mile upstream.

The pools in the gorge can leave you with almost no place to go except backward or straight up. I usually visit Ripton Gorge with my good friend Bob Adams, one of the most experienced outdoorsmen I know. He has told me of times when a sudden shower raised the river level a good four inches in less than a half-hour. This kind of current change can be extremely dangerous and anglers would do well to travel in pairs when making their first descent into the gorge.

In fact I recommend that anglers wishing to fish in Ripton Gorge for the first time seek out a friend who has a good deal of experience there to accompany them. I would also advise folks who are in less than good physical shape not to attempt the trip. While the lure of exceptional fishing is a great one, the many dangers associated with the heavy climbing and hiking could be disastrous for the unprepared. Ripton Gorge will make you pay for every lovely wild trout it yields. Having warned you of all the gorge's many perils, I'll discuss the strategies for fishing it.

To begin with, your selection of equipment will be quite a bit different from that for a normal fishing trip. While most experienced anglers know that a pair of waders fitted with felt soles are vital to a safe and successful wading effort, at Ripton Gorge I suggest you forgo waders in favor of a good pair of sneakers. If you wish, you may fix felt to the bottoms of your sneakers, but it is far more important to have rugged soles for climbing the rock ledges and boulders which surround the river at the bottom of the gorge. In other words do not worry about what lurks beneath the water's surface so much as about what looms above it.

Next, while I personally prefer to fish tight pieces of trout water with a fly rod, you may wish to approach the gorge with an ultralight spinning rig. Casting room is at a premium in Ripton Gorge, especially along the top three-quarters of a mile. Quite often an angler will find himself casting to a beautiful deep pool filled with foot-long rainbows from a ledge located a good ten feet or more above the river.

Once, while I was fishing the gorge with Bob Adams, we crept up on a likely-looking stretch of water only to find that it was completely inaccessible to us. I considered moving out along the rock ledge we were standing on, past this run, to cast into the pool above it. Bob would have none of that. With the casual indifference of a true gorge veteran, he cast his $1/12$-ounce Phoebe lure from our perch into the upper reaches of the run. On his second cast Bob hooked into a fat, leaping rainbow of about 13 inches.

Would that I could give you a truly accurate account of this fabulous fish. It jumped clear out of the water upon being hooked and rushed downstream toward us. I ducked under Bob's arms as he swung the rod tip around to counter the fish, while he reeled madly to keep up with the charge. The fish jumped again, this time moving off to our right. Bob countered again by dropping the rod tip as the trout jumped and began to double back toward us once more.

The fish began to tire, and Bob started to muse upon the real problem he faced. How was he supposed to get the exhausted rainbow up to where he and I stood? Our moving down to the fish was completely out of the question, as we were standing on top of a rock face a good ten feet above where the trout lay thrashing in the water. Unfortunately our decision was made for us as the rainbow took one more run and managed to work the hook out of its jaw.

Anglers will find that several of the best stretches of water in Ripton Gorge flow between steep rock formations. In fact one very deep pool which holds some nice-sized brown trout is blocked from the upstream side by the presence of a huge natural bridge. This lovely rock opening also prevents the angler from moving farther upstream, unless he or she is willing to climb up the gorge walls and around the bridge. It is impossible to wade under the bridge, as the water which flows beneath it is swift and deep.

The most effective way to fish the gorge, then, is to work from the westward, or downstream side, toward the east. Hike along the water's edge, using the prominent boulders and cliffs to hide your approach. The water is very clear in the gorge, and it washes free of silt quickly after a heavy rain. Also, while the gorge may fill rapidly during a rainstorm, it will also drain with equal speed. This means it can be fished shortly after drenching rains, when many other rivers near it are high and muddy.

Fly-anglers can fish the gorge, in spite of my advice to the contrary at the beginning of the chapter. However, there are a few things you should know before trying it. First, because the descent into the gorge is so sharp, it would be wise to bring a 3- or 4-piece pack rod, strapped to your back in its carrying tube. There are plenty of places along the winding access trail where a hiker might fall and accidentally snap his or her rod tip off against a tree or the forest floor. Also, you will want to have your hands free during your descent to break your fall, should you experience one.

Second, because backcasting room is so scarce in the gorge, be ready to roll-cast a lot more than you might ordinarily. The rock ledges and giant boulders can easily snap off the end of the hook on your fly. You also might prepare yourself for the disappointing experience of having to pass up some of the deeper holes in the gorge. Many are completely inaccessible to fly-anglers.

Finally, because falling from the top of one of the ledges or rocks is quite likely, it is wise to bring a fly rod and reel which are, for lack of a more delicate phrase, "expendable." I would offer the following story to illustrate this point.

I took my ultralight spinning rod and camera down into the Ripton Gorge to try to get some photos for this book. It is one thing to describe the natural bridge at the upper end of the gorge, but it is quite another to actually show you just how remarkable this rock formation is. I have climbed through several gorges with my rod and camera before, and while there is always a certain risk in doing so, I have been lucky for the most part.

I was approaching the final five hundred yards of my trip and was beginning to tire. While climbing along a rock formation on the northern shore, I slipped and fell hard on my left leg against a ledge jutting out about five feet below where I had stood. My shin began to

The view upstream from the downstream end of Ripton Gorge. Anglers should approach the Gorge by proceeding upstream from the small bridge on VT 125 which crosses the Middlebury River just east of East Middlebury.

swell and turn an ugly dark-red color, so I hobbled down to the stream to get it in the water to reduce the inflammation and pain. After five or ten minutes I felt I was ready to move on.

The truth of the matter was, I had done some substantial damage to my leg and was in a lot more trouble than I thought. It became harder and harder for me to climb and maneuver between the rocks as I headed upstream. By the time I reached the two pools just below the natural bridge, I was in real pain and was having a great deal of difficulty. Still, I figured that if I could just get into position to take one good photo of the bridge, it might all be worthwhile.

As I moved past the lower of the two pools still separating me from the picture I wanted, I had to climb over a large boulder and up along a ledge, and then I had to prepare myself to slide down the far side of the rock face. I was simply unable to keep my grip on the rock and began a long, graceless slide down the rock and into a deep pool of water below.

The water felt kind of nice, actually, but my camera went in too, and the photo session was in vain. The episode brought home to me the lesson that it is wise to pack along only the barest of necessities when visiting this beautiful and fruitful fishing location. You may wish you had brought your best graphite ultralight or tiniest bamboo fly rod once you have first descended into the gorge and started to fish, but further exploration will bear out my premise.

Anglers wishing to experience the fun of fishing the Middlebury River without risking loss of limb and property should consider the very upper and lower stretches, instead of Ripton Gorge, for their outings. There are plenty of good fish to be had throughout this water.

9

The Mad River

The Mad River is an unusual stream because it runs from south to north, hence its name. It runs alongside VT 100 from its brooklike beginnings in Granville, through the towns of Warren, Waitsfield, and Moretown. It finally empties into the Winooski River near US 2 in Middlesex. Twenty-three small brooks feed the Mad along its twenty-nine-mile path. Most notable of these are Lincoln and Freeman's brooks in Warren, and Shepard and Mill brooks, which run through Fayston and Waitsfield.

If we use the main tributaries as landmarks, the Mad River can be broken up into four main sectors: the upper, which consists of the waters upstream of Lincoln Brook to the river's source in Granville; upper-middle, which takes in the river from Lincoln Brook north to Mill Brook; lower-middle, or from Mill Brook to Shepard Brook; and the lower, which runs from Shepard Brook to the river's mouth.

The dominant species in the upper portion of the river is the native brook trout, although there are some populations of wild rainbows present as well. The rainbows make their way here during their spring spawning run. They do not normally venture upstream of the area midway between Lincoln Brook and Stetson Brook, but they do keep themselves busy in the deeper, fast-moving water downstream. This stretch of water, only one mile long, is one of the most fertile pieces of trout water on the Mad.

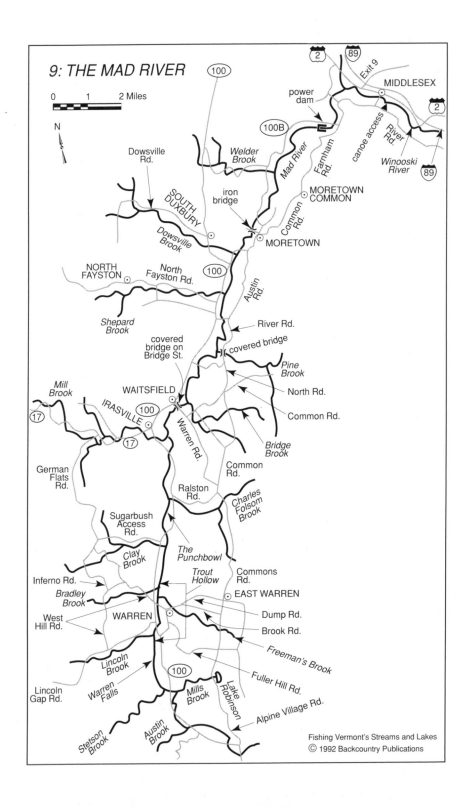

9: THE MAD RIVER

0   1   2 Miles

N

MIDDLESEX

Exit 9

power dam

canoe access

River Rd.

Winooski River

100

100B

Welder Brook

Mad River

Farnham Rd.

Dowsville Rd.

SOUTH DUXBURY

iron bridge

MORETOWN COMMON

Dowsville Brook

Common Rd.

MORETOWN

NORTH FAYSTON

North Fayston Rd.

100

Austin Rd.

Shepard Brook

River Rd.

covered bridge on Bridge St.

covered bridge

Pine Brook

Mill Brook

WAITSFIELD

North Rd.

IRASVILLE

100

Common Rd.

17

Warren Rd.

Bridge Brook

17

German Flats Rd.

Common Rd.

Ralston Rd.

Charles Folsom Brook

Sugarbush Access Rd.

Clay Brook

The Punchbowl

Commons Rd.

Inferno Rd.

Trout Hollow

EAST WARREN

Bradley Brook

Dump Rd.

West Hill Rd.

WARREN

Brook Rd.

Freeman's Brook

Lincoln Brook

100

Fuller Hill Rd.

Lincoln Gap Rd.

Warren Falls

Mills Brook

Lake Robinson

Alpine Village Rd.

Stetson Brook

Austin Brook

Fishing Vermont's Streams and Lakes
© 1992 Backcountry Publications

The upper river is notable for two things. As the Mad continues its northward flow, it passes through an area which is both promising and yet also very frustrating for anglers. This stretch holds some of the prettiest and most productive native brook trout and wild rainbow water on the river, but it is also one of the most heavily posted. During the early 1980s, landowners along the Mad began to post their property more and more, until by the end of the decade roughly half the land access to the river had been covered with NO TRESPASSING signs. Almost all of this small upstream section above the mouth of Lincoln Brook has been posted, although there are several places where anglers may get to the stream from VT 100.

Only a mile downstream from the entrance of Stetson Brook is a series of pools and waterfalls known as Warren Falls. This is a privately owned piece of land which has been the subject of local controversy since the middle 1980s. For years swimmers, hikers and anglers made use of this beautiful spot until the landowner decided to post it.

The waters upstream from Warren Falls must be fished with the very lightest of gear. The heavy forest growth along the banks forms a canopy which keeps most of the river in constant shade. It is necessary to cast under tree limbs and over fallen logs to get at some of the best pools and runs in this area, and this is best done with a short rod, under 7 feet in length. A 3- or 4-weight line complements this outfit, and anglers would be well advised to use a short leader, say 6 feet long. Downstream from the falls and all along the river until you hit the mouth of Lincoln Brook, you may want to use the same type of rig, or you have the option of switching over to slightly heavier gear. The last couple of hundred yards of this section are a bit more open, and the fish here can be somewhat larger, in the 10-inch range as opposed to the 6- to 8-inch fish you will find farther upstream.

There is relatively little wind on the upper Mad River, as the forest growth is quite dense. You will also find a small beaver pond situated above the river, just upstream from the mouth of Lincoln Brook. Both the still air and the pond contribute to a healthy insect population. Hatches of biting insects like black flies and mosquitoes are quite common during May, June, and early July along this part of the river. Mayfly hatches are also very common during the early portion of the trout season through June.

The first prime fishing location on the second quarter of the river is in Warren village itself at a place known as Trout Hollow. The river travels right through the center of the village, and while there are numerous buildings situated along the shoreline, there is virtually no commercial development. Accordingly, the water quality here is good, supporting healthy populations of rainbows and brookies.

The river is slow-moving and flat as it heads into the village. This is the first part of the Mad where anglers are apt to hook into recently stocked fish. These stocked trout are usually rainbows, and they will stay in this calm water. This is due to the fact that a small dam stands here which a homeowner has converted into a hydropower generator. The house itself is remarkably large, and the sluice gate leading into the turbine is fenced off by a large grate. While the fishing above the grate is spotty, below the dam, where the water runs much more swiftly, anglers will find rainbows in the 10- to 12-inch range. Footing along the river banks is sometimes very difficult, and anglers will have to bushwhack through the woods on occasion to get from one pool to the next. Wading can be tricky too, as the river bed drops off abruptly, forming deep pools.

The fishing remains productive as the river leaves Warren village. The two-mile stretch between the village and the Sugarbush Access Road holds some nice rainbows, although the number of brook trout declines. Anglers will also come across the first good brown trout water here. Like most trout streams, this piece of the river is best fished from downstream, so anglers might wish to spend a day hiking along from where Clay Brook enters the river up to Trout Hollow. The wading is fairly easy until you hit the lower part of the hollow, and there are some tremendous pools which are home for some of the river's largest rainbows and browns. This area is, however, heavily posted.

The upper middle of the Mad is not a stretch that can be fished throughout the season. In fact, outside of the months of May, June, and September, the section of river between the lower part of Warren village and Clay Brook is not all that productive. Up until the river leaves the village, it is canopied by forest growth. Shortly thereafter the river is exposed to open air for the first time. Water temperatures in July and August can be much higher here than they are upstream. Obviously, there is also a shortage of shady areas for trout to hide in.

However, fly-anglers can do very well in this part of the river by making longer casts with large attractor flies like Royal Humpies or even Muddler Minnows. With the Muddler, try allowing it to swing past you and drag across the current downstream. The brown trout seem to have a strong appetite for this kind of offering. You may want to use heavier equipment than you were working with above Warren village. The big pools are slow moving, and the fish in them have every opportunity to observe new additions to their environment. The lack of cover has some positive effects on fishing, though, particularly early in May. The direct sunlight warms the water and the air around it, creating a perfect medium for large insect hatches. Cream-Colored Cahills are common, and the rainbows can be seen rising during midday for these emerging insects.

Seven- to eight-foot, 4- or 5-weight rods are the order of the day in this piece of the Mad. You will also want to use at least a 7½-foot leader with a 2- to 3-pound tippet. Spin-anglers should do well too. The best bet is an ultralight with 4-pound-test line. The most deadly lure seems to be the Phoebe, a small gold, copper, or silver spoon shaped like a fish

An angler kneels to avoid being seen by a pair of spawning rainbow trout on the Mad River in early spring.

with an S-shaped curve bent in it. The gold-colored lure has always done best for me, but the copper one often works just as well.

As the river flows north from the mouth of Clay Brook, it passes under an iron bridge and curves away from VT 100 behind Kingsbury's Country Store. Anglers will find recently stocked trout here mixed in with the wild population of rainbows. The number of browns begins to jump here too, as the river widens and deepens. This one-mile section of the river receives quite a bit of pressure from area anglers, although few of them venture out of sight of the bridge. Therefore the more intrepid wader/hiker can do well by following the river into the trees.

In fact there's a very good strategy for fishing this stretch of the upper-middle river. Start fishing about three-quarters of a mile downstream from the bridge and work your way toward it. The wading is fairly rugged, so be prepared to leave the stream occasionally to avoid falling into the deeper water. While fly-anglers will do well here, a spin-angler with an ultralight will have a great time casting from the shoreline. This is not easy footing, however, either in the river or along the shoreline.

In 1989 the Sugarbush Ski Resort unveiled plans to construct a large water-storage lagoon here to build up the area's snow-making capabilities. The plan was to divert water from the Mad at a point just behind the Kingsbury Country Store into the lagoon with a runoff channel to be dug just downstream. This project received approval from the state environmental commission during the summer of 1991. At the time of this writing it was unclear what effect this development would have on the river. Both the state and federal governments will be watching the progress of this water diversion carefully for any possible effects it might have on trout life.

Below the runs behind the country store, the river flows through a series of large pools called The Punchbowl. The Punchbowl is a popular swimming hole, and during the warm months of June, July, and August the fishing is not very good, as the sunbathers and swimmers drive off most of the fish. However, as the river flows northward, the stream narrows, and the angler finds a series of pools and small runs which extend for almost three miles, sometimes traveling through some beautiful but steep rock formations. The river passes along the western side of VT 100 and maintains a healthy distance from it throughout this section.

About halfway down this three-mile stretch, Charles Folsom Brook enters the river from the east. The area which comprises the hundred yards or so downstream from the mouth of the brook is very productive brook trout water, for the fish use the cool waters of the brook to set up their domain. There's good brook trout fishing in the brook as well, although this is tough fishing with anything but the shortest of fly rods, given the heavy tree growth along the brook's banks.

Between the brook and the spot downstream where the highway crosses over the river near a country inn and a small roadside diner is perhaps the best piece of brown trout water in this part of the Mad River. There are few buildings along the shore, and they are spread out over great distances. The water runs deep and fast here with a pattern of rapids, runs, pools, and then long stretches of shallower water before the next grouping of rapids, runs, and pools. This is also prime rainbow water, although you will find lots of mature brown trout here in the fall. The water is fed by several small springs, so the river will support some brook trout as well.

From the bridge on VT 100 near the Lareau Farm Inn, which crosses the river just before Irasville village, the shore of the Mad River becomes more crowded. You are now entering a business district, and the water quality suffers, although not too badly. You won't find many brook trout here, but you will find some fairly good fishing. Access is very easy, as the river passes close to the road and to the various retail businesses. Most business owners are glad to let you fish off their shorelines, but be sure to check with them before you take to the water.

Mill Brook enters the Mad River just behind the Austin Sheep Farm. Immediately downstream, as the river enters the village of Irasville, the river cuts away from the highway and into a wooded area behind the commercial and residential buildings there. Despite the proximity to so many structures, the piece of water between the brook and the town recreation field gets relatively little fishing pressure.

The stretch just past Irasville has two popular swimming holes, but the water between them is not well used or traveled. Stocked rainbows and browns work their way into this area from the covered bridge on Bridge Street in Waitsfield village. You will find some good-sized brown trout holdovers and some smaller wild rainbows as well, particularly in the deep holes at the lower end of this section.

Heading downstream from the covered bridge, anglers will find

The power dam located just four miles from the mouth of the Mad River.

increasingly promising water in the lower-middle quarter of the Mad. Strangely, most anglers seem to like to stay close to an easy access area and rarely explore much more than the 50 to 100 yards immediately up or downstream from that point. The wading downstream from the covered bridge is fairly easy, too, which makes this behavior all the more mystifying. Most of this is pocket water, small pieces of water which run about two to four feet in depth mixed in with the much shallower main flow. Some good rainbows live here. Where Pine Brook enters from the east about two miles later, you will find another one of those isolated populations of native brook trout.

The 1½-mile stretch between Pine Brook and Shepard Brook is perhaps the most heavily fished piece of the Mad River. The Department of Fish and Wildlife stocks this part of the river frequently during the spring. The river is much deeper and wider in this section. In fact it begins to wind around in an aimless way. The best opportunities for good brown trout and rainbows are in those spots where the river swings farthest from the highway. This part of the river is quite open, surrounded by dairy farms and cornfields.

The mouth of Shepard Brook enters from the western shore, near the point where VT 100 meets the North Fayston Road. Shepard Brook is a staging area for spawning brown trout. The water surrounding the mouth of the brook is well known to most anglers and is a favorite fishing spot of many of them. However, the fishing is tough here, as the river is very open; the sunlight during the summer makes this area virtually hopeless. It is during the early and late parts of the trout season that the half-mile around the brook's mouth is most productive.

The lower-middle Mad River is wide and deep enough to warrant the use of fairly heavy gear. Rods of 5- and 6-weight and of a length up to 8 feet are standard, as the fly-angler is quite apt to hook into fish well over a foot in length. While the average size of Mad River trout is only 10 inches, anglers have a good chance at something larger here. Spin-anglers can still do well with 4-pound-test line, but they might want to consider switching to 6-pound, especially if they choose to venture even farther downstream into the lower river.

The river continues to snake its way downstream toward Moretown village, winding through several large farms. The two miles between Shepard Brook and the bridge that crosses the river just south of Moretown village is not fished much and is quite productive. The section between Shepard Brook and Dowsville Brook is hardly fished at all, since it passes almost out of sight of the highway. This is fairly big water, especially for a small river like the Mad, and there is little cover, making fishing during the summer months unproductive. However, during May, June, and September the brown trout and the rainbows are very active, and anglers would do well to wet a line here.

As the river enters Moretown village, it pours through a narrow gorge which quickens the current considerably. This is excellent rainbow water, although it does receive some pressure, especially during the summer. The high rock formations cast long shadows across the river and its rapids, allowing trout some badly needed cover. Caddis imitations and terrestrials seem to be the most effective baits. The wading is difficult here, which gives an adept fly-angler with hip waders a decided advantage over anglers who prefer to stay close to shore. This gorge empties into a deep pool which is a favorite of sunbathers and swimmers during the summer.

The river flows on the western side of the highway through the village. After a short, open section, the river enters another gorge. Again the river is narrowed and its current picks up. The footing here is extremely tough, as the river flows through the small gorge and over a tiny dam into another open area. As the river leaves the village, it flows under an iron bridge and into a heavily wooded stretch. This portion of the river is not heavily fished, and for approximately a mile the river travels through a sparsely populated region which holds some fine rainbow trout fishing. Fly-anglers can cast confidently here, because while there is plenty of shade for fish to hide in provided by the trees on the high banks, there are few overhangs to snag your backcast.

The highway crosses the river again about 1½-mile north of Moretown village, and here the character of the river changes dramatically. With only a few exceptions, access to the river is very good for the next 3 miles, and the fishing pressure is enormous. While the small stretches of unfished water offer an occasional oasis for the angler seeking trout, they are spread out, and that makes fishing in this area difficult.

Just four miles from the mouth of the river there is a power dam which empties out into a series of very long rapids and another gorge, just a mile downstream. This last stretch of the river is perhaps the most promising for the adventurous angler, as it holds not only some very large rainbows and browns, but smallmouth bass as well. During the spring the smallmouths run up out of the Winooski River and into the Mad to spawn. However, this is primarily trout water.

Fly-anglers will want to use their heaviest gear here. Nine-foot rods of between 5- and 7-weight are advised, and anglers would do well to tie on tippets of no less than 3-pound test. The Royal Coachman is king here, and I have found that even the most ardent adherent to the match-the-hatch philosophy will switch to this bizarre attractor pattern. It pays not to argue with what works, and the Coachman is deadly.

Where the river finally empties into the Winooski, anglers should consider using a canoe to fish this wide, slow-moving stretch of water. Good-sized browns will hole up next to the large boulders that fill the bottom of the river, and it is almost impossible to reach them either from the shore or by wading.

10

The Dog River

The Dog is not a large river, but it does hold some nice trout. Anglers fishing the Dog would be well advised to approach the river cautiously, as many of the large browns and rainbows make their homes in the deeper, slower-moving stretches of the river. They will be able to detect your movements in the water very easily, so I suggest you try making your first casts to a new pool from the shore before venturing into the water for a better angle.

The river begins in Roxbury and heads north along VT 12A. Fed by several small brooks at the town's northern end, this stretch of the river is best known for its brook trout fishing. The Dog is very small here, and this pattern of small-stream fishing with tiny brook tributaries extends until the river finally winds its way past the Northfield Country Club and Norwich University. While the brookies and browns anglers encounter through this area are apt to be only 6 to 10 inches in length, the upper part of the Dog River is also host to a fairly good-sized spawning run of these two species during the fall.

Access to the upper river is quite good, although anglers will have to do some hiking off VT 12A, particularly behind the university. This is a scenic area, though, and the view alone is worth the small inconvenience. Fly-fishing can be difficult. The river is overgrown with heavy tree growth, and these limbs often appear to work as magnets for the luckless fly-angler who is not careful about his or her backcast.

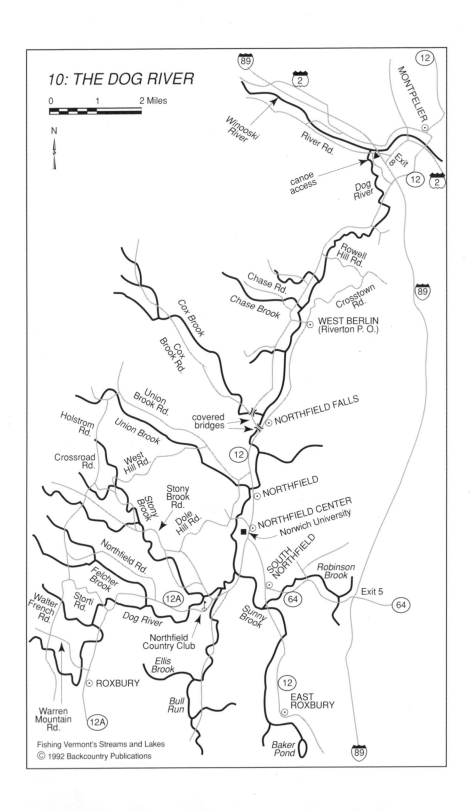

10: THE DOG RIVER

0   1   2 Miles

N

89
2
MONTPELIER
12

Winooski River

River Rd.

Exit 8

12
2

canoe access

Dog River

Rowell Hill Rd.

Chase Rd.

Chase Brook

Crosstown Rd.

89

Cox Brook

Cox Brook Rd.

WEST BERLIN
(Riverton P. O.)

Union Brook Rd.

Holstrom Rd.

Union Brook

covered bridges

NORTHFIELD FALLS

Crossroad Rd.

West Hill Rd.

12

Stony Brook Rd.

Stony Brook

Dole Hill Rd.

NORTHFIELD

NORTHFIELD CENTER

Norwich University

SOUTH NORTHFIELD

Robinson Brook

Northfield Rd.

Felcher Brook

Walter French Rd.

Storti Rd.

12A

Dog River

64

Exit 5

64

Sunny Brook

Northfield Country Club

Ellis Brook

12

ROXBURY

EAST ROXBURY

Warren Mountain Rd.

12A

Bull Run

Baker Pond

89

Fishing Vermont's Streams and Lakes
© 1992 Backcountry Publications

This giant brown trout is typical of the huge fish that lurk in the Dog's deeper holes and longer runs. Perhaps it is a relative of Dizzy's!

But the most important story on the Dog River starts once you have left the settlement that makes up downtown Northfield and the river begins to widen as it moves northward toward its mouth at the Winooski River. The fishing for big browns and rainbows is tremendous. Also, given that the state rarely stocks this section of the Dog with rainbow trout, the fishing for truly wild trout is exceptionally good.

The Dog River enjoys the reputation of being one of Vermont's premier brown trout streams. I have seen more browns over the 18-inch mark on this one stream than on any other I have visited. In fact, during the summer of 1991, I became totally fixated on one particular mile of this river and the enormous fish that live in it.

I first spotted him on July 1. I had just finished guiding a trip which saw my client bag a huge, 22½-inch, 4-pound brown and was bringing him back along the river bank to where I had parked my truck. As we walked on a ledge that looked down on the river, I saw something move out of the corner of my left eye. After scanning the water some fifteen feet below us, I saw him.

He was gorgeous. A giant brown trout, well into the 2-foot-long range with dark spots all along his side and a huge, gaping white mouth. I stopped my client and pointed down into the water. Soon he was gaping like the fish as he realized that this monster eclipsed the beauty he had caught himself just a half-hour before. And so my summer was spent looking at this fish, my fish, trying to figure out a way to catch him. Every time I guided this piece of the river, I looked for the fish. And every time I did, he was there, looking every bit as majestic as he did the first time I saw him.

I took Larry Pyne, the outdoor sportswriter on the *Burlington Free Press,* fishing on the Dog and again I searched for my fish. As usual he cruised into view after a few minutes and began his ever-repeating tour of his domain. Larry told me he thought my obsession with this trout, regardless of his great size and enormous beauty, was unhealthy.

"The next thing you know, Pete," he warned, "you'll have a name for him, and everything."

Hah! I thought. That will never happen to me. But as I drove home from that fishing trip, listening to the radio, I realized that my fish did resemble someone who had given me a great deal of joy over the years. With his cool demeanor, his entertaining antics, and that huge mouth: he looked just like jazz trumpet legend Dizzy Gillespie.

And so now my fish had a name: Dizzy. I went back to the river and fished it with one of my guides, just to show him some of the better pools in case he had to guide there later that season. But instead of starting the trip by showing him where the best accesses were and what to look for in the long, deep pools and runs, I headed straight to the ledge and looked for Dizzy. I could not begin the day without knowing how this, my newest of friends, was doing. And there he was, cruising about the pool at top speed, chasing the black-nose dace which he fed on. My guide and I spent almost a half-hour watching him until finally the guide couldn't stand it any longer.

"Are we going to cast to him?" he asked impatiently.

"Do and you're out of a job," I growled back. "That's *my* fish!"

Dizzy is still there, terrorizing the smaller fish like some aquatic dictator. I still go down to see him every time I fish the Dog, although the strong bond between the two of us prevents me from trying to catch him. Someday, though, I will go down to the pool to scan its depths for Dizzy and he will not be there. I only hope he succumbs to old age, having lived to be the largest trout in the river.

I first fished this particular piece of the Dog, near the Northfield/ Berlin town line, with Brad Fortier, a new friend of mine who has spent many years fishing the Dog. Brad and I have tromped around the river in Northfield Falls, Riverton, and downtown Northfield catching and releasing large numbers of small rainbows, browns, and brook trout. We use three types of lures when we spin-fish, which is Brad's favored method of catching trout: number-2 Mepps, ⅛-ounce Phoebes, and Brad's favorite, a number-11 Rappala. Brad employs a strange, jerking motion in his retrieve of this giant lure, and while it only produces a few strikes on each trip, it normally causes a couple of huge brown trout to emerge from their hiding places to see what all the fuss is about.

The big browns tend to lurk in the slower-moving long pools that are scattered throughout the length of the river. The water on the Dog is

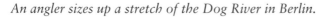

An angler sizes up a stretch of the Dog River in Berlin.

crystal clear, and this allows these giant fish an enormous advantage in that they can easily see any intruder coming before it has had a chance to become a real threat. These big pools are generally quite far apart, so you will have to hike up to five hundred yards to get from one to the other.

The fishing is like this all along the Dog River. You will also find nice runs with a little whitewater bubbling at their tops which will be filled with rainbow trout in between the big pools. These runs are best fished with a fly. While spin-anglers will be able to cast to and bring in fish from these small, fast-moving pieces of water, they are far more apt to spook the fish than anglers using dry flies on the surface.

Working up these runs is pleasant enough for most anglers. The river rarely gets very wide or deep, and wading is easy. There are a few exceptions to this rule, though, particularly in the area of Berlin known as Riverton. A beautiful gorge in this part of the stream holds some large brown trout and rainbows. However, the wading is anything but easy here. Anglers are forced to work their way slowly along the edge of the river, grasping the sheer rock ledges alongside to keep from falling into the deep water, which slopes away suddenly from these outcroppings.

While getting through the gorge can be tough work, a clever angler will find many good places to stand and cast. Fly-fishing is not impossible in this area, although I would suggest that you bring a fairly light rod of short length. You will need at least one hand free at all times to steady yourself while you travel along the ledge, so you will not want anything cumbersome on you to impede your progress. I worked this area with a small fly rod and my bulky camera and its 200-millimeter lens one day and found it was very difficult going. I might have been much happier if I had left that camera at home, giving me one less thing to worry about.

A remarkable point to keep in mind while fishing on the Dog River is that it is paralleled by both VT 12A and VT 12 as well as the Central Vermont Railway. The railroad crosses the river no less than fifteen times, and these crossings provide some very interesting angling opportunities of their own.

Railroad crossings are never places to be taken lightly. They are dangerous and should be treated accordingly. Once while guiding two clients on the Winooski River near the town of Bolton, I noticed two young anglers on the shoreline opposite me. They were having a tough day, losing several good fish while getting very few strikes. After an hour I watched them pack up their gear and head into the woods. A few minutes later one of my clients came running over to me, excitedly pointing downstream. A tall railroad bridge crossed the river there, and the two young anglers I had been watching were slowly walking across it, a good sixty feet above the water's surface. We all held our breath as the pair worked their way to safety. No more than two minutes later the Central Vermont Railway shook as the regular freight run from the north ran over the bridge. Our foolhardy friends had missed certain disaster by an extremely narrow margin.

Still, while railroad bridges are not places to play on, they are very good places to fish under and around. The many railroad bridges that cross the Dog River have formed some deep long pools for big fish to inhabit. The natural erosion caused by the water driving around the concrete buttresses has provided an ideal place for good-sized browns to hide. You will often find them pressed right up against the ledges and drop-offs where the concrete widens to form a deep pool. The fish love the protection these large structures offer as well as the shade they cast during midday.

Unlike regular road bridges, railroad bridges do not attract the weekend angler with his can of worms and bobber. Most folks are smart enough to recognize the danger of walking across railroad bridges and will stick to the safer spots near the road. However, the angler who either does not mind getting his feet wet or wears a good pair of waders can hike in to the places where the rail lines intersect the river.

The Dog bears to the west as it approaches the city of Montpelier with the railroad following its path toward Montpelier Junction. As it tucks in behind the Montpelier recreation field, you will find that an increasing number of anglers come to fish the river. The access is easy, and you are quite apt to run across several groups of people working this piece of water during June and July after work lets out at five o'clock.

As the Dog finally reaches the Winooski River, the first-time visitor will notice a surprising thing. While this piece of fine trout water has traveled almost twenty miles, it has maintained an almost uniform width and depth except in its first five miles. It is still the same small

Waterfalls can hide some truly enormous trout. Here at Northfield Falls, an angler casts to rising rainbow trout.

river it was back in Northfield Falls and in Riverton.

This uniformity is one of the three remarkable points which make this river such a classic trout stream. The second is the surprising depth and length of its big pools, already described. These are key to the survival of the big fish that live in this river. But the third attribute that marks this river is even more important: it will clear up from the heavy silting of a big storm faster than almost any stream in this region, allowing anglers to get back on the water quickly while the big fish are still active.

It is no secret that the largest brown trout in any river become most active just after a good rainstorm. However, the high water and discoloration of the stream can make fly-fishing extremely difficult. The Dog, like any river, receives a healthy dose of mud and runoff during a storm, but it will run clear within hours of such a downpour.

I took two sets of clients on consecutive days up the same stretch of the Dog, near Northfield village one day in late August. The first crew got halfway up the mile we were fishing when it began to rain. By the time we reached the end of the piece we wished to work, we were in a drenching storm, and we ran back to my parked truck. We sat and watched as the river level rose and the water turned brown.

By the next morning, while the river was still running quite high, the discoloration had greatly eased. By the time my two clients and I had reached the big pool where my clients from the day before had been when the storm began, the water was already running close to clear. As we cast our fly lines into the river, big brown trout began to rise all around us, feeding on the terrestrial insects that were being washed off the shore. Rivers like the Mad, Winooski, and New Haven all ran silty that day, and the Winooski remained murky for two days after that. Only the Dog was fishable the day after the big storm.

One last note: While the Dog contains a demonstrably strong population of wild rainbow trout and some of the largest browns I have found anywhere in the state, it is also a fragile ecosystem. An accidental chlorine spill from the Northfield municipal swimming pool killed thousands of Dog River fish in 1989. The Vermont Fish and Wildlife Department decided against restocking the half-mile stretch of river affected by the spill, hoping that the river in time would heal itself. In fact, after only two years at this writing, this piece of the Dog River once again supports trout and seems well on its way to a full recovery.

One should not mistake this rejuvenation as indicating some super-resilience that the Dog River possesses. Rather, consider that the Dog, like any river, has the ability to clean itself by its natural flow and that trout will always return to a healthy environment. But this river is a delicate balance of influences, many of them man-made. Any abrupt shift in that balance can cause catastrophe, like the chlorine spill in 1989.

I would therefore urge anglers to practice catch-and-release fishing here. The Dog River boasts some fabulous trophy browns and some equally astounding rainbows, but instead of keeping your monster fish and having it stuffed to be mounted on your office wall, might I suggest that you bring a small pocket-sized camera along and photograph it before you release it?

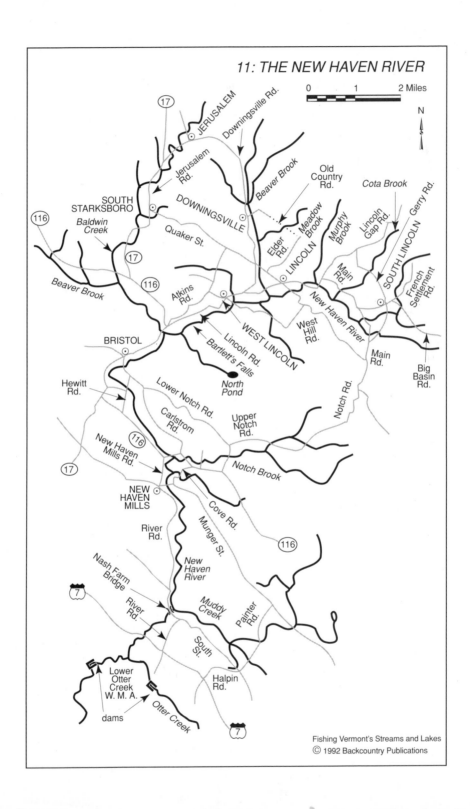

11: THE NEW HAVEN RIVER

0   1   2 Miles

N

(17)

JERUSALEM

Downingsville Rd.

Jerusalem Rd.

Beaver Brook

Old Country Rd.

Cota Brook

Gerry Rd.

SOUTH STARKSBORO

(116)

Baldwin Creek

DOWNINGSVILLE

Meadow Brook

Murphy Brook

Lincoln Gap Rd.

Quaker St.

Elder Rd.

LINCOLN

Main Rd.

SOUTH LINCOLN

French Settlement Rd.

Beaver Brook

(17)

(116)

Atkins Rd.

New Haven River

WEST LINCOLN

West Hill Rd.

Main Rd.

Lincoln Rd.

BRISTOL

Bartlett's Falls

North Pond

Notch Rd.

Big Basin Rd.

Hewitt Rd.

Lower Notch Rd.

Carlstrom Rd.

Upper Notch Rd.

New Haven Mills Rd.

(116)

(17)

Notch Brook

NEW HAVEN MILLS

Cove Rd.

River Rd.

Munger St.

(116)

Nash Farm Bridge

New Haven River

(7)

River Rd.

Muddy Creek

Painter Rd.

Lower Otter Creek W. M. A.

South St.

Halpin Rd.

dams

Otter Creek

(7)

Fishing Vermont's Streams and Lakes
© 1992 Backcountry Publications

11

The New Haven River

The New Haven begins its thirty-mile run in Lincoln, a small town on the west side of Lincoln Mountain. There are several small tributaries here which make up the headwaters to this trout stream, the best known being Cota, Murphy, and Beaver brooks. The river tumbles down the mountain and meets a major natural obstacle at Bartlett's Falls in the neighboring town of Bristol. It then heads into the village of Bristol and takes a sudden turn to the south into New Haven township, where it feeds into Otter Creek.

This is a great piece of trout water, and all three species of river trout are available to anglers who wade through the many riffles, runs, and pools that make up the complexion of the river. The New Haven was once thought to be such a fine trout stream that a wild trout catch-and-release stretch was designated in the town of New Haven. This experiment has unfortunately met with far less success than was hoped. I will deal with this story when I get to that particular length of the river

First, though, let us discuss the upper portion of the New Haven, as it runs off Lincoln Mountain into Bristol. The whole area upstream from Bartlett's Falls is populated with native brook trout. This is a beautiful area, filled with lots of runs, pools, and riffles which are home to many small- to medium-sized fish. Getting to the river can be half the fun too, as you will have to travel on the Lincoln Gap Road, which is one of the steepest grades I know.

You approach the gap from one of two directions. If you are on the western side of the Green Mountain Range, in the Champlain Valley, you get to the road via VT 17/116, right where it crosses the river on the stone bridge at the big curve in the road at Rocky Dale, 1½-miles out of Bristol village. Instead of heading north on VT 17/116, you head up the mountain. The gap road is marked with a yellow sign warning you that winter travel is inadvisable. You will also see signs directing you to Lincoln and the nearby town of Warren.

The other way of getting to Lincoln Gap Road is via VT 100 as it first enters the southern end of the Mad River Valley and the town of Warren. As you head north on 100, you will see a small service station and signs pointing to Warren village on your right. To your left, or on the west side of the highway, Lincoln Gap Road is a steep paved route which is marked with the same ominous sign warning against winter travel that you will find on the Bristol side.

In either case you must make your way to Lincoln on the Gap Road to begin your fishing trip on the New Haven River. Lincoln is a lovely town which features some extraordinary views of the countryside to the west of the Green Mountains. The river is not much larger than a small brook at this stage, but it is loads of fun here to pick your way from rock to rock with a light fly rod in search of the small native brookies. These fish are rarely all that particular about what they feed on, but Cahills, Hendricksons, and Adams seem to work best. You also might try mosquito imitations, as you are apt to run across a lot of these annoying little beasts while you wander through the woods.

As you head down the mountain toward your rendezvous with the falls, the river widens, and by the time you leave the village of Lincoln and are about halfway to the intersection with VT 17/116, you should be able to cast a slightly larger fly rod with little difficulty. The fish get a bit larger too, although you will find that most run at about 8 inches.

The area immediately above and below Bartlett's Falls is popular with the swimming and sunbathing set. Accordingly, fishing here during the middle of the day is not great. It seems most of the sun-worshipers arrive on the scene at around ten or eleven o'clock in the morning. They will normally pick up and leave at around six in the evening. This still leaves you lots of time to fish, especially when the weather is warm. The fishing slows down anyway as it gets close to noon.

Bartlett's Falls itself is extremely dramatic. The falls cascade down over a rock cliff which is at least three stories high. The pool below is quite deep, and you will first run into the river's many fine brown and rainbow trout here. Shortly after you pass the falls, you will see VT 17/116 as the river heads toward Bristol village.

VT 17/116 crosses the river twice in brief succession before you hit the outskirts of the village. On this stretch you will find the river on the south side of the highway. It is a great-looking piece of water, filled with rocks and boulders which offer plenty of good places for trout to hide. The only real drawback is that access is almost too easy, and lots of folks fish in here, especially near the two bridges. However, I can promise you that the early-rising angler will do well in here, using stoneflies, midges, and attractor patterns.

As the river heads abruptly south in Bristol village, your best access will be a back road out of the center of town called Lower Notch Road. This road gives you plenty of good places to get out and wade into the river. However, the abundant access does not last for long. When Carlstrom Road enters from the west, the river heads west too. Carlstrom Road bends about two miles along the eastern shore of the New Haven until it runs into VT 116.

This is a terrific stretch of the river, partially because it is a little off the beaten path, but mainly due to the fact that the road only crosses the river once in the entire three miles. As I have mentioned before in this book, anglers do not seem to like hiking very far from their cars to get to productive trout water. Because there are so few ideal accesses to the river here, the fishing can be awfully good if you do not mind walking a bit.

The river has the usual pattern of pools and riffles which distinguish this stream. In fact I have to admit that few Vermont trout streams have as consistent water conditions as the New Haven. There is one riffle after another and plenty of good, deep pools at the river's many bends.

The other way of approaching this section of the river is via VT 116. You can either take Hewitt Road off Lower Notch Road, which affords you access to a short piece of the river's western shore as a dividend, or you can bypass Notch Road entirely. Instead, stay on VT 17/116 until 116 separates and heads to the south. Take VT 116, and you will see the river to the east in about a mile. The advantage to taking VT 116 here is that it gives you a more direct route to New Haven Mills

View of the falls at Rocky Dale on the New Haven River.

Road, which enters the highway on the west side. This back road, and Cove Road just to its south, are your two best ways of keeping up with the river down to the bridge which marks the upper border of the catch-and-release section I mentioned at the beginning of the chapter.

In 1983 the 3½-mile stretch between the bridge where Munger Street crosses the river five miles south of Bristol village to the Nash Farm Bridge near where Muddy Branch enters the main stem was established as a voluntary catch-and-release area. This was initiated by the New Haven River Anglers Association, a local group which asked that all anglers fishing this piece of the river join their effort. The following year the state Fish and Wildlife Department stopped stocking the catch-and-release area, making it a wild trout stretch. In 1987 a new regulation was introduced by the state that backed up the New Haven River Anglers Association, mandating catch-and-release fishing on the 3½-mile piece of the river. Furthermore, the state ordered that only artificial lures and flies could be used.

In 1991 a report was written by the state which recommended an end to this experiment. State fisheries biologists concluded that the area in question was not able to support a wild trout population due to lack of sufficient pool habitat and in-stream cover for fish to hide in. Water temperatures in the catch-and-release area were measured in the midseventies during August, and it was observed that few trout inhabited the stretch of river in question during midsummer. However, this has not ended the Fish and Wildlife Department's efforts to establish catch-and-release trout waters in the state. The search is still on for other suitable rivers.

Nevertheless, some very interesting data were obtained as a result of the catch-and-release experiment on the New Haven. Between 1986 and 1989 Fish and Wildlife performed electroshock surveys on the river in order to determine the viability of the fishery as a wild trout stream. As the experiment on the catch-and-release stretch needed monitoring, it was decided that extra attention would be paid to this area. Therefore, of the seven sites in which survey work took place, two were in this area.

What the state fisheries biologists learned was that the two most productive areas for wild trout fishing were near the mouth of the river and at the big bend just to the west of Bristol village. The first of these two areas was estimated to hold 349 trout per square mile, a fairly impressive figure. But more extraordinary were the findings near Bristol. It was estimated that the concentration of trout there was 762 fish per mile, more than double the population at the river's mouth.

The numbers for the rest of the river are equally interesting. The entire catch-and-release area accounted for some of the lowest averages in the survey. Only 197 and 177 trout per mile were estimated to be living in the two test sites in this piece of the river. Only the area just upstream from the catch-and-release stretch showed a lower density of trout population.

The survey also sampled the waters of Baldwin Creek, a tributary on the upper third of the river which meets the main stem just east of Bristol village. This tributary was estimated at 256 trout per mile, which is quite impressive for so small a piece of water. The area downstream from the confluence of Baldwin Creek and the river was estimated to hold 296 trout per mile.

So, while the catch-and-release experiment on the New Haven proved to be a failure, the river itself will probably bring any angler heading out for it a good deal of success. The estimates I have just quoted attest to this, as does the gorgeous habitat itself. Fly-anglers should have great luck here using the patterns I have already described, while spin-anglers might want to work the water with small spoons. The main tributaries of the river, Baldwin Creek, Notch Brook, and Muddy Branch's experience some decent spawning runs in the spring and fall as well.

From the bottom of the catch-and-release section to the mouth of the river where it meets Otter Creek is productive water, far more so than the area immediately upstream from it. According to state Fish and Wildlife Department estimates, your chance of hooking into a wild trout in this last little stretch of water is nearly double that in the preceding 3½ miles. The habitat is considerably better, and you will find an abundance of rainbows and browns here. Access is best via South Street, which runs into River Road just before the stream takes a hard turn to the west to Otter Creek.

Don't forget to check out Muddy Branch while you are fishing down here. If you stay on South Street southbound, it will turn into Halpin Road, which is your best route to Middlebury. But the real draw for me is the creek, which runs alongside the Halpin Road until it intersects with Painter Road. Access is good, and the fishing for brookies, browns, and rainbows can be excellent.

12

Winona Lake (Bristol Pond)

The town of Bristol is located along VT 116, about midway between the city of Burlington to the west and the Mad River Valley to the east. Apart from the fine New Haven River, perhaps the most interesting piece of water located in Bristol township is Winona Lake.

The lake sits at the northernmost part of town, just below the border Bristol shares with the town of Monkton. It is a small body of water, only a mile long from north to south, and a half-mile across at its widest point near the lake's center. A small brook enters from the south, feeding the lake. Another stream, Pond Brook, flows out of the northern end of the lake and eventually winds its way into Lewis Creek in southern Hinesburg.

Winona Lake is a superb fishery, with healthy populations of bluegill, yellow perch, bass, and northern pike. Because pike and bass are warm-water fish, they thrive in the hot weather of midsummer that causes so much suffering for trout. They are powerful swimmers and can pull out enormous amounts of line once hooked. An average-sized bass for Winona Lake runs in the 1- to 1½-pound range, while the average pike will run three times this size; 6- to 10-pound northerns are not uncommon.

The northern and western portions of the lake are unapproachable by foot, as they are covered with swampland. In fact the only access for anglers is via Pond Brook at the northwest end, and then only by boat or canoe. The Department of Fish and Wildlife maintains a road and

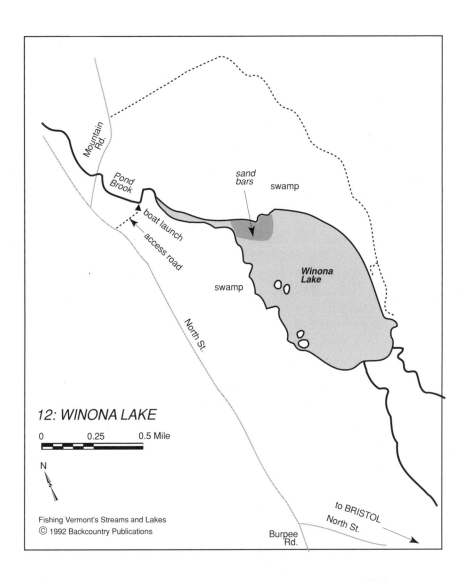

12: WINONA LAKE

0   0.25   0.5 Mile

N

Fishing Vermont's Streams and Lakes
© 1992 Backcountry Publications

boat access area there which accommodates small craft only. Given the size of the lake, large boats and power engines are not necessary for weekend anglers to reach good fishing.

The fishing on Winona Lake is good almost all the time during early spring through the fall. In fact ice-anglers do well here during the winter months as well. But the most exciting fishing takes place right after ice-out in late March and early April, when the northern pike come into the shallows to spawn.

Because Pond Brook flows from out of the northern end of the lake, this piece of Winona Lake tends to freeze up late. Similarly, the northern quarter of the lake is the first to ice out in the spring. Once ice-out takes place, the mature northern pike begin to move into this area to begin their spawning ritual and to feed.

Northern pike like weedy, muddy waters, and while the lake will not have grown its normal, midsummer crop of weed until June or July, there will be a sufficient amount of rotting vegetation from the year prior present during the early spring to make them feel at home. During late March and on into April, the northerns will congregate in large numbers at the bay where Pond Brook begins. They are highly aggressive fish and will often spar among themselves for territory and mates. This activity offers some great fishing opportunities for the fly- or spin-angler who is lucky enough to chance upon it.

Canoes are the preferred method of travel on this lake. Even though the water may betray the frantic activity below the surface, these fish can easily be spooked or distracted by unnecessary or unnatural movement. Canoeists are apt to see huge swirls and splashes on the water as the northerns jockey for space, food, or mates, and much of this surface activity is apt to be in the main channel of the brook itself. Therefore, stealth upon one's approach to the northern bay is a must.

The shoreline of the brook is a dense scrub which hides fish waiting in ambush for their next meal as well as root systems and branches which lie in wait for the angler's lures or flies. It is important to cast accurately along the shorelines, as you are just as likely to catch a snag as a good-sized pike. I will tend to use somewhat heavier than normal line when fishing here. A 6-pound-test monofilament for open-faced spinning gear or a 4-pound-test tippet for fly lines seems to work quite well, although I recognize some anglers may wish to use even heavier line. A 6- or 7-pound northern heading at full speed into a weed bed or one of those two brook shorelines can put a terrible strain on fishing line.

I prefer an 8½-foot, 6-weight fly rod with a 4-pound tippet when I fly-fish for northerns or a medium-action, 6½-foot spinning rod with 6- or 8-pound-test line. I do not use a steel leader with either of these types of tackle in spite of the sharp teeth these fish possess. I have found that the use of leaders and swivel snaps actually does not help me very much.

Swivel snaps and steel leaders tend to interfere with the natural motion a lure is designed to imitate. Leaders add extra weight which results in a larger splash, while swivels impede the normal action of most spoons, spinnerbaits, and crankbaits. Granted, swivels allow the angler to change lures rapidly and also prevent the fouling of the line. However, I still urge you to avoid them when fishing with spinning tackle.

To those who feel the need for a quicker lure-change than can be accomplished by cutting the line off one lure and tying on another: I wonder what your hurry is. If you knew you were trading the proper action of your lure for a few extra casts, would you bother? Remember, anything between your fishing line and the lure you have chosen impedes the movement that lure was designed to imitate. One well-placed and efficiently retrieved cast past a feeding fish is much more likely to produce results than several unnatural retrieves made in rapid succession, no matter how many different lures you use on a given day.

I will admit that spinning lures cause a twisting of the line and promote the eventual fouling of that line in the reel. But the fact that swivels alter the natural motion of the lure more than outweighs any advantage they might offer in keeping your line untwisted. I received some very good advice on this subject from a friend of mine, Jerry McKinnis, the producer of the long-running cable television program *The Fishin' Hole*. He pointed out that the easiest way to avoid having your line get fouled in the first place is to change it often. In fact Jerry changes his line every time he goes out fishing. While this approach may prove prohibitively expensive for many anglers, I think the point is well taken. Monofilament line is easily twisted or nicked, so when you go out to do battle with big fish like northern pike, you should make sure your equipment cannot be blamed for any failure you might experience.

While Winona Lake is best known for its fine northern pike fishing, bass anglers will enjoy the lively largemouth that inhabit the weedbeds and tangles of roots along the shorelines.

This is especially true when you fish Winona Lake and encounter those big pike and largemouth in the northern bay and in Pond Brook. These fish will take to the dense cover almost immediately after they have been hooked. When this happens, there are two things you should do. The first is to stop the fish's run. The second is to turn it out into the main body of the lake. If you are fishing with a companion in your canoe, have him or her steer your end of the canoe to the deeper water and begin paddling in that direction. Make sure you do not move too quickly or too abruptly, as the combination of the fish's surge and your sudden movement may be enough to break the line. Instead, hold the fish firmly in position, exerting pressure while your friend gently coaxes it in the direction you choose. Once out in open water, have your companion hold the canoe in as close to a fixed position as possible while you work the fish in.

If you are fishing Pond Brook itself, you have a distinctly different problem on your hands. To begin with you will be working in extremely close quarters, as the brook is rarely more than thirty feet wide. If your fish runs into the brushy shoreline, your best bet for success is to have your friend paddle the canoe toward the fish while you maintain line pressure. Sometimes the fish will work itself loose while you do this. If so, keep paddling toward the moving fish and keep applying as much pressure as you can. Northern pike do not tire easily, so any advantage you can coax out of your equipment and the ability to move to the fish with your canoe should be used.

Boating a pike is an interesting process in itself. The easiest way to do this is to use a large landing net. Dip it completely underwater and work the fish's head over it. Once the fish is in position, lift up the net, and the pike will slide in. If your northern is too big for the net, grasp the fish by the tail, lift it straight up out of the water and into the canoe. While some anglers I have fished with prefer to take the northern pike by grasping its head, using its eye sockets as holes to grip with, I advise you to keep your hands far away from the fish's mouth. Northern pike have very sharp teeth and extremely powerful jaws. While I have never lost a finger to these critters, I certainly have been painfully bitten more than once.

Having boated your northern, you must be careful when extracting the lure or fly from its mouth. While surgical forceps are always a good idea for this task, you also might want to bring along a pair of heavy pliers. Pike have bony mouths, and your hook is apt to be deeply embedded in the jaw rather than in the fleshy part of the lip. Work the hook out gently, and your fish will be ready to be released. Even though northerns are hardy fish, they still will require a fair amount of time and attention before they can safely swim off.

Bass require somewhat different treatment. Like pike, largemouth bass love to work their way into obstructions and break your line by wrapping it around sunken logs, roots, or rocks. You have to be particularly careful of this along Winona Lake's shoreline. Finally, in boating your bass, a net isn't always necessary. Bass do not have the sharp teeth pike do, and they can be easily lifted out of the water by grasping the lower lip with your thumb and forefinger.

Pike and bass will range over the entire lake during the late spring and through the summer into fall. I have seen them chasing schools of perch out by the island in the middle of the lake in June and July or cruising the small coves of the eastern and western shores during September and October. Fishing for them in midsummer is a challenge, as they like to dive to the bottom of the lake to feed on perch and small minnows. This activity helps to keep them out of the bright sunlight and the excessive heat. Like most fish, pike become a bit sluggish as the temperature rises, but they are easily roused into action.

Spinning flies, streamers, and lures will provoke northern pike into feeding activity. The use of spinning attachments on artificial flies and streamers is quite common among salmon-anglers, and these devices work equally well on pike. Let your spinner settle down to a depth of about 6 feet—8 to 10 feet if the weather is especially hot—and retrieve with an even, slow to moderate pace. If the fish do not react, speed up your retrieve and occasionally halt the spinner so that it stalls and begins to drift back down to the bottom again before continuing your reeling.

Spoons like the Silver Minnow are also effective pike attractors. Most often these lures are trolled from the back of a slow-moving canoe at a depth of at least ten feet. However, anglers can also catch northerns by casting spoon lures into weed beds and retrieving them quickly along the top. Pike and good-sized bass love to sit at the edges of these weeds to wait for a likely-looking meal to swim by. They also enjoy the shade and cover these areas offer them.

Winona is a great spot for bass. During May when the largemouth are spawning, you will find them congregating along the same bay where the pike were in March and April. However, they will not be limited to this area as the pike are in the early spring. There are numerous shallows and mounds throughout the lake which the large-mouth call home. The mounds and underwater humps which cover the lake floor are also the locations for the lake's heaviest weed growth.

Winona Lake is filled with lots of the types of underwater structure that bass love. There are several shallow sandbars along the eastern shore which are home to large numbers of mature largemouth. Some of these bars are in sheltered areas which are perfect breeding grounds for aquatic insects like mosquitoes, black flies, caddis, and mayflies. During the first big insect hatches of May and June, bass can be seen taking these emerging insects right off the surface during the middle of the day. However, most of the bass surface activity is restricted to the late afternoon and early evening hours when the sun has begun to go down, air temperatures have started to cool, and the wind has died.

May and June are a fly-angler's dream on the lake, for that is when the mature bass spawn and enjoy that first major feeding period since the previous autumn. Surface-fly patterns like the Elk Hair Caddis and Olive Drab, and heavy-hackled flies like the Yellow Humpie can be deadly. But you should be willing to experiment with less likely patterns too. After all, these fish are at their most primal, hyperactive state during spawning. In short they will hit almost anything. I have taken 2- and 3-pound bass at Winona Lake on large, number-10 stonefly nymphs and Woolly Buggers during the late spring. There did not appear to be any nymphs or flies on the water that looked like these two patterns on those days in question, but the fish were in such a frenzy that they hit anyway.

Bass are territorial fish, and when they dig out their nests for spawning, they become even more so. All along the shallow shoreline on the east side of the lake and in the channel of Pond Brook, the largemouth are digging nests, laying eggs, fertilizing them, and then protecting their domains. Remember, it is illegal to keep bass during the spring spawning season, although you may catch and release bass in Vermont from the second Saturday in April until the opening day of bass season two months later.

The western shoreline of Winona Lake is good bass water too, especially for spin-anglers with a love for spinnerbaits. Spinnerbaits are large, clumsy lures which have the unfortunate characteristic of landing on the water with a great deal of splash and noise. For this reason I have never been terribly partial to them. Having said this, I would add that I have had terrific success with them at Winona Lake on both bass and northern pike.

If you fish along the western shore, you will find long sections of the lake that hold good-sized bass and northerns throughout the year. The important factor in locating those fish, especially the bass, is looking out for weed beds, points, and submerged structures like logs and other debris. This is a fairly common-sense approach except for one thing: the fish react quite differently to these structures during different times of the year. During the spring I will buzz a spinnerbait at full speed along the top of the water right over a weed bed and find that the bass attack it with great enthusiasm. A few weeks later, as temperatures rise, this tactic will work better on pike. Later still, say in late June, I will have to fish these same spots with slow-moving spinnerbaits, cranked six to eight feet below the surface in order to get a strike. As the heat turns up in July and August, the spinnerbait must be carefully bounced along the bottom and at an extremely slow speed to attract a cruising bass or northern.

This brings up another interesting point about bass and pike. Bass tend to congregate during most of the year, while northerns appear to live more solitary lives. I have noticed that if I get a nice-size bass by casting near a sunken log, my next cast into that same area is apt to produce another, similar-size fish. However, if I take a good northern on a lure or a fly at a particular place on the lake, subsequent casts to that same point rarely are productive. The exceptions to this rule occur during spawning season in the early spring or when a group of pike are herding a school of perch or bluegill during a feeding frenzy.

These gluttonous feasts are fearsome to watch. The smaller fish are driven into the air in their desperate attempts to escape being eaten. The only sights I have seen that are quite like it are the huge blitzes of bluefish you will see on the Atlantic Ocean in late September and early October as the blues corral giant schools of menhaden and butterfish. The biggest difference is that while the bluefish will attack their prey and often only eat a single mouthful of a given fish, the northern pike will almost always eat the entire fish. A pike will take its food in its mouth by the tail and run with it until the smaller fish is subdued. Then the pike turns the fish around and swallows it head first.

I would like to add two notices of caution regarding Winona Lake. The first is that access without a boat or a canoe is next to impossible. The lake is surrounded by swamp. Naturally, the various species of predatory birds like kestrels, owls, hawks, and ravens live here comfortably, but most land animals steer clear. Moose have been spotted from time to time at Winona Lake, but this is a fairly rare occurrence.

The second point is that because the shore is densely infested with poison ivy, you should be careful about approaching the lake from any point except the Fish and Wildlife Access, and even here caution should be exercised. Poison ivy, as a rule, does not survive well in the northern and central parts of Vermont, but Winona is one of the exceptions to the rule. I have even gotten the irritating itch and rash of exposure to the frozen rotted leaves of this plant during the dead of winter when on one of my infrequent ice-fishing expeditions to the lake. If while fishing you decide to come ashore anywhere except right at the boat-launching area (which is itself covered with poison ivy, so don't wander far away from well-trod paths and clearings here either), keep an eye out for poison ivy low to the ground and climbing along tree trunks or bushes.

13

The Winooski River

The Winooski is one of the three major tributaries to Lake Champlain that we will deal with in this section, the other two being the Lamoille and the Missisquoi. It is a large river, with deep holes and fast-moving rapids. Canoe enthusiasts and kayakers love this river for its fast-moving flow and challenging runs. Similarly, anglers will find its fishing very impressive. Not only will you find good populations of smallmouth bass and brown and rainbow trout, but you will also encounter runs of steelhead, landlocked salmon, and walleye.

The landlockeds and the steelhead are found toward the lower portion of the river, downstream from a place known as The Salmon Hole. The Salmon Hole is located near the Champlain Mill Shopping Mall in Winooski. During the spring and then again in the fall, landlocked salmon will run up out of Lake Champlain toward the dam in an effort to spawn. Steelhead, in smaller numbers, will often accompany the salmon during the spring. This whole part of the river is restricted during this time. Between April 1 and June 1 of each year, anglers may not fish along the area from the bridge on Routes 2 and 7, upstream to the downstream side of the railroad bridge that crosses the river just to the east of Exit 15 on I-89. There is a large power dam at the top of this stretch of the river, and the salmon like to spawn in this area.

It is important to note that the whole section of the Winooski from Bolton Dam in Bolton to the Lake Champlain boundary is open to

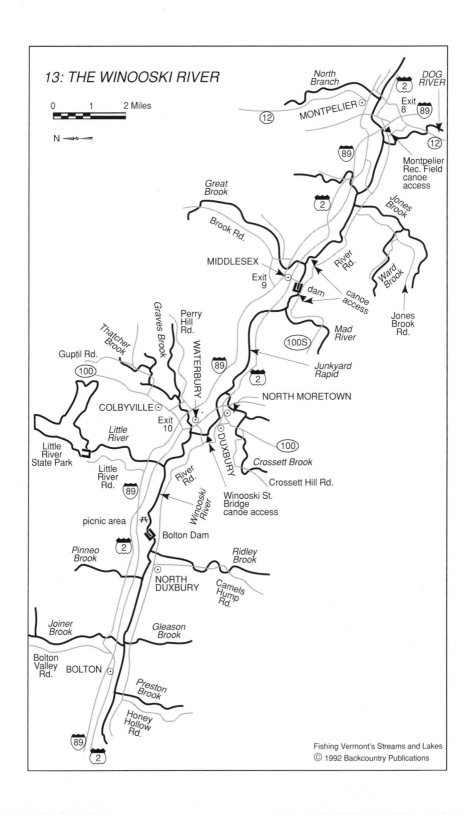

13: THE WINOOSKI RIVER

0   1   2 Miles

N

North Branch

DOG RIVER

MONTPELIER

Exit 8

Montpelier Rec. Field canoe access

Great Brook

Brook Rd.

Jones Brook

River Rd.

MIDDLESEX

Exit 9

dam

canoe access

Ward Brook

Jones Brook Rd.

Mad River

Graves Brook

Perry Hill Rd.

Thatcher Brook

Guptil Rd.

WATERBURY

100S

Junkyard Rapid

COLBYVILLE

Exit 10

NORTH MORETOWN

Little River

DUXBURY

100

Crossett Brook

Little River State Park

Little River Rd.

River Rd.

Winooski River

Crossett Hill Rd.

Winooski St. Bridge canoe access

picnic area

Bolton Dam

Pinneo Brook

Ridley Brook

NORTH DUXBURY

Camels Hump Rd.

Joiner Brook

Gleason Brook

Bolton Valley Rd.

BOLTON

Preston Brook

Honey Hollow Rd.

Fishing Vermont's Streams and Lakes
© 1992 Backcountry Publications

fishing twelve months of the year. The catch is, you may only fish here for species like perch, walleye, bullhead, and pike during the late fall and winter months. These fish are legal all year long on streams that the state does not designate as "closed trout waters." There are very few of these year-round pieces of river in the state, so it is important to take note of the ones which feed into Lake Champlain. They are:

- *Lamoille River*: From the Central Vermont Public Service Co. power dam at Fairfax Falls in the town of Fairfax to the Lake Champlain boundary.
- *Missisquoi River*: From the Rixford Manufacturing Co. dam in East Highgate in the town of Highgate to the Lake Champlain boundary.
- *Otter Creek*: From Center Rutland Falls in the town of Rutland to the Lake Champlain boundary.
- *Poultney River*: From the CVPS dam at Carver Falls in West Haven to the Lake Champlain boundary.

The view from "Hugo" of the Middesex Power Dam on the Winooski River.

While the lower Winooski may have a great deal of appeal, especially because of its generous open season, I would like to spend the bulk of this chapter describing the middle portion of the river, which runs from where the Dog River enters the Winooski near the city of Montpelier downstream to just below the Bolton Dam.

The four- or five-mile stretch of the Winooski that flows from the Dog River to the Middlesex Dam is extremely easy to canoe and holds some very good fish. In fact, since almost all of this area is flat and slow-moving, the best way to fish it is by canoe, rather than by wading. The river can run deep, although you will find large holes separated by hundred-yard-long stretches of shallow water that are not very productive. To reach this part of the river, take Montpelier Junction Road, a small, paved piece of road located right under I-89 in Montpelier. Take the last right-hand turn off the entrance ramp to the interstate before I-89 North. This road will lead you under the interstate and to a point where Dog River Road enters on your left. Take Dog River Road and the Montpelier Recreation Field will appear on your right in a few hundred yards. The field is an ideal place to park your car, unload your canoe, and access the very bottom of the Dog River as it slides into the Winooski. Or you may make the short portage down to the banks of the Winooski from here.

Anglers can troll their spinning lures and streamer flies along these shallower sections, but they should use care. It is very easy to snag your line, as the floor of the Winooski is covered with rocks both large and small. These make good places for a hook to attach itself, and while the current is not so strong that it will be difficult to return to the place upstream where you have become hung up, it is inconvenient.

Perhaps the nicest run via canoe is the nine-mile stretch of the Winooski between the Middlesex Dam and the long, shallow section to the west of Waterbury village. If you decide to take the first float trip I have suggested in this chapter, you will have to pull your canoe out of the river just upstream from this dam. Some adventurous folks may wish to continue the journey downstream, but be warned that it·will take you about 3½ hours to fish from Montpelier to Middlesex. It will take you another 6 hours to fish the river from the dam into Waterbury.

There is a great canoe access just below the Middlesex Dam which allows you to get right on top of the good fishing almost immediately. The first rapid you will encounter is a gentle one named Hugo. Between the dam and Hugo is some fine rainbow fishing, and anglers should spend a little time here before starting their downstream travels. The high rock cliffs which dominate the scenery along the northern bank drop off into the water sharply, creating a natural ledge where smallmouth bass love to congregate. When the water is being pushed through the power dam, the downstream water level can be a full three feet higher than when the power turbines are shut down.

When the water is low, the trout, bass, and fallfish begin to emerge from the depths and will feed along the top. Trout and the rare 16- to 18-inch fallfish will take number-14 and -16 White Wulffs and various parachute patterns during June, July, and August. The bass, however, are most vulnerable to number-1 and -2 Mepps lures and plastic grubs on ⅛-ounce leadhead jigs. The whirring blades of the Mepps or even of a Rooster Tail lure will attract bass beautifully. The jigs are effective especially during the middle portion of the day when the fish tend to lie in the deeper parts of the river.

Another highlight of this nine-mile run is the Junkyard Rapid, which appears about halfway between the dam and the most accessible pull-out near the Winooski Street Bridge in Waterbury village. Anglers who have not run the Winooski River before might wish to land their craft and take a few minutes to look over this rapid before proceeding. It is a deceptive stretch of water. The first chute forces the canoe sharply to the right, but the sternman must be ready to steer the canoe immediately to the left after passing through this fast-moving bit of the rapid. There is another benefit to taking a break here at the Junkyard Rapid: deep holes along the rock formations hold some good-sized rainbow trout.

Shortly after the Junkyard Rapid, anglers will encounter an island. This island is downstream from a public parking access where anglers may also launch and land their crafts. This access is notable for its large pine trees and a scattering of picnic tables.

As the angler gets closer to the village of Waterbury, the river flattens out considerably. There are some good, deep holes to fish here, and there is also a large bridge on US 2 which spans a wide, deep section of the river. The bridge marks the easternmost part of the village and serves as a marker. In just a shade over a mile, another bridge will appear. This is the Winooski Street Bridge, where there is a logical access for landing a canoe.

Between the Winooski Street Bridge and the Bolton Power Dam lies a 3½-mile piece of river which holds some excellent rainbow and brown trout. While this area can be fished by canoe, there are no practicable places to pull yourself out of the river before you reach the dam. Most of the river runs far away from the road, and the few places where the road and river do come near each other feature some very steep and difficult banks. Therefore I prefer to fish this part of the Winooski with fly gear, wearing waders.

There is, however, one exception to this last statement. You can pass by the Winooski Street Bridge and continue downstream by canoe to the point where the Little River enters, about 1½ miles later. There is no easy place here to remove a canoe, either, but anglers will find an enormous advantage at being able to hang right at the mouth of this smaller stream, particularly if the Little River is running low. If the Little River is running high after a recent rainstorm, however, anglers would do well to avoid this tactic, as it will be next to impossible to

Two canoeists set up to negotiate a small rapid on the Winooski River just upstream from the Junkyard Rapids.

navigate a canoe around the mouth of the river.

I guide a lot of trips on the Winooski River in Bolton. This area is the last we will discuss in this chapter. The section of the river that runs from the Little River to the Bolton Dam is best reached by wading. River Road runs parallel to the river along the southern shore, and there are many good places to get into the river as you follow it west out of Waterbury.

Perhaps the most popular stretch of the Bolton section of the river is the one-mile piece just below the dam. The outflow of the dam has created a very large pool which is a well-known place for early walleye fishing during March and April. Anglers will also do well fishing for smallmouth bass and brown trout here during May and June. Fly-anglers will want to use heavy gear, either 6- or 7-weight, and heavily weighted flies like Woolly Buggers or Black-Nose Dace.

The walleyes are best caught on spinning gear. I have found that using 3- or 4-inch plastic grubs on ⅛- or ¼-ounce jigs work very well, as do all manner of spinning-blade lures like Panther Martins or Mepps. Cast your lure upstream and crank it back toward you slowly. The walleye is not a beautiful fish, but it will fight hard and is absolutely delicious if you broil it over a wood fire.

Another good area to explore is about a half-mile downstream from Bolton Dam, near North Duxbury. You will encounter some very big water here, as well as some truly amazing fish. The river is wide, perhaps 100 feet across, and up to ten feet deep. Huge rock formations create some furious rapids which empty out into some of the largest runs and pools of the river. This is challenging water to fish, and it can also be quite hazardous to wade. However, this North Duxbury segment of the Winooski becomes productive earlier in the season than many other nearby rivers.

I took three young gentlemen from Puerto Rico fishing on this stretch one spring. The air temperature was about 55, and the river was running about five degrees cooler. However, we soon noticed there was a sizable mayfly hatch going on. Swallows were swooping all over the river's surface feeding on these emerging insects, as were a healthy population of rainbow trout. The fish were lying in the calm backwater behind large boulders and in protected inlets, waiting for food to drift past them. In spite of the relative cold of the water, these trout were very active.

Using attractor patterns like Royal Wulffs and Humpies, I success-fully caught several of these rainbows, while the three clients I was guiding did quite well with brown trout using weighted Woolly Buggers at a dead drift. I told them to fish this ugly little fly with a small piece of split shot attached to the leader, up about eighteen inches from the end. As the piece of shot hopped along the river bottom, it dragged the fly behind it, causing it to take a zigzagging path up and down the river bed. This realistically imitates the action an emerging nymph exhibits as it crawls out from under the safety of the rock it has been living on and heads to the surface. Brown trout find this movement irresistible, and they took the offering with characteristic zeal.

My three fishing partners also did quite well using ⅛-ounce Phoebe lures fished at a depth of about two feet and cranked in at a slow speed. The browns tended to follow the lure for several yards before striking, as is their custom. Brown trout are very wary creatures and were slow to initiate an attack. The rainbows, however, were less careful and often took the small spoon within seconds of its landing in the water.

One final tip on the Winooski would be for you to get on the river as it passes the mouth of Joiner Brook, near the Bolton Valley ski area. The bottom half-mile of this little stream is a staging area for spawning brown trout during the fall. Be sure that you wade through the brook itself if you decide to fish the northern shoreline of the Winooski here. The dense growth along the shore of the brook holds large amounts of poison ivy, and a quick hike through it can ruin your whole fishing trip.

14

The Little River

When the thermometer hits the nineties, as it does during late July and August, fish living in rivers and lakes have an awfully tough time of it. The rising water temperature causes their own blood to heat up and also lowers the oxygen level in the water, making them sluggish and inactive. Particularly hard hit are the region's trout, which prefer water temperatures of between 50 and 65 degrees.

For the summer angler, therefore, it becomes vital to locate water that falls in between these readings. But if the air temperature is running closer to 90 than to 65, where to look? The answer is really quite simple: you go to reservoirs and fish the outflows of the power dams. We have such a place at the Waterbury Reservoir. The water that flows out of the big dam that creates the reservoir and into the Winooski River three miles downstream is called the Little River. Because the water is drawn from the bottom of the dam, it runs at an average temperature of 52 degrees, perfect for trout fishing.

And the fishing is very good in the Little River. It is a small piece of water, except when the power turbines are in operation at the dam and the water runs high. It also has some very deep pools and several long, productive runs where rainbow and brown trout thrive. During the opening week of the trout season, browns in the 18-inch range are taken out of one very large hole at the top of the river. During the warm summer months, big browns are also taken at night and right at dusk on Woolly Buggers by fly-anglers working the deeper portions of the

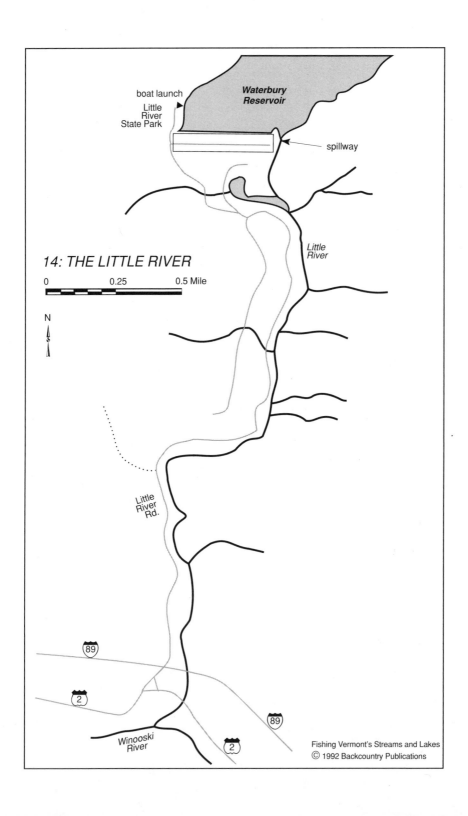

boat launch
Little
River
State Park

*Waterbury
Reservoir*

spillway

*Little
River*

14: THE LITTLE RIVER

0   0.25   0.5 Mile

N

Little
River
Rd.

89

2

89

2

Winooski
River

Fishing Vermont's Streams and Lakes
© 1992 Backcountry Publications

river. This is not easy fishing, but the payoff can be spectacular.

Morning anglers have their best luck using small Adams flies and stonefly nymphs. These folks are on the water by seven o'clock at the latest and leave the river by ten or eleven. Interestingly enough, the water in the Little River is so cool that you may feel as though the surrounding air is not quite as hot as it really is. I fished the Little River with a client from New Jersey once on a particularly hot, sticky day, and we felt that the temperature on the water's surface was a good fifteen degrees cooler than it was up on the road where we had parked my truck. This wasn't actually true, but the water flowing about our legs as we waded through the river kept us comfortable in spite of the oppressive heat. The trout seemed to enjoy the climate, too, and we caught several brook trout that were rising to a hatch of small midges. We saw some very nice rainbow trout as well, but were unable to coax them into striking at our flies.

The Little River is a short piece of water, barely three miles long from where the flow originates at the Waterbury Reservoir Dam to where it empties into the Winooski River. But because the flow of this river is regulated by the outflow of the power dam, it offers some unique fishing opportunities.

Hydroelectric dams work on the simple principle of water being forced through turbines to generate the necessary friction to create an electric current. The more water pushed through the turbines, the more power produced. However, when rainfall is scarce, the dams will hold more and more water back each day to allow for maximum power production once sufficient pressure is built up. It is during these holding modes that anglers can best take advantage of the dam to catch fish.

Big trout, especially browns, happen to love living in the tailwater created by power dams, chiefly because the water pushed through the turbines is often much cooler than the normal flow. This is especially welcome during heavy droughts like the one experienced in Vermont during the summer of 1988. Guiding became very difficult for me and my staff, as most rivers experienced extremely low water flows and abnormally high temperatures—in the high seventies and even the low eighties. We took clients to the Little River regularly that year and found the cold water there kept good-sized rainbows and browns active even during the worst of the drought.

This brings us to the second major reason why tailwater fishing on the Little River is so productive. When water is being run through the dam's turbines to generate power, the downstream water level is very high. Fish will tend to stay down deep, avoiding the extra turbulence. However, as soon as the dam stops producing power and the downstream levels start to drop, the fish will begin to become much more active. Another effect from the water's dropping after the turbines shut down is that the receding waters downstream from the dam create an artificial low tide. This in turn stirs up the river bottom, loosening food sources like stonefly and caddis nymphs from the rocks they attach themselves to. Once this takes place, trout will often feed wildly.

Fly-anglers will have a distinct advantage when fishing during this period, for the really big trout will be feeding almost exclusively on nymphs as they are swept into the current. Whenever you fish tailwater, though, be careful to keep your eye open for changing water levels. The level can go up by as much as three or more feet in just a few minutes once the power dam starts up its turbines. It is very easy to find yourself trapped out in the middle of the river with nowhere to go for safety. Thankfully, this is less of a concern on the Little River than on a larger river like the Winooski, which also has good pieces of tailwater to fish.

Most of the Little River is accessible via the Little River Road, a small dirt roadway that heads north off of US 2 just to the west of Waterbury village. There are several pull-overs for motorists along the road, and for the most part these are logical places for you to begin your fishing trip. However, as you head upstream, you are apt to find that wading becomes difficult once you have traveled several hundred yards, due to the river's numerous deep holes. Similarly, you will find that the terrain of the shoreline leaves something to be desired for easy hiking. But this is part of the reason why this tiny stretch of water is so productive: much of the river is difficult to get to and receives little or no fishing pressure.

There are many places for the angler without mountain goat-climbing skills to fish on the Little River, including several convenient spots where a driver may pull over and either hike through the woods to the bank or climb down into the river from a steep incline. You are apt to notice that these areas have easy-to-find paths that lead you to the river. While this does mean that you will begin by fishing right at a well-traveled spot, if you wander a few hundred yards either up or

A fly angler casts upstream to a riffle on the Little River.

downstream, you will eventually work your way out of the better-known pieces of the river and into some productive trout water.

The river bed is a rocky, gravelly piece of terrain, and the footing can be a bit slippery. The river runs slightly discolored as of this writing, as a result of a bad flood during July of 1990. There were two major storms during that month. During the second storm, a great deal of muck was washed out of Stevenson Brook on the reservoir and into the area where water first enters the turbines. This muck has settled and continues to leach through the system. There has also been a fair amount of erosion along the shoreline of the upper part of the Little River, and this sediment continues to work itself downstream.

However, anglers should not be overly concerned with this discoloration. The Little River's water may be a trifle muddy, but it is still very clean. You will find plenty of healthy brook trout throughout the length of the river, testifying to the purity of the water.

The river is also the site of a major run of spawning brown trout during the fall months. Big browns, often in the 18- to 24-inch range, move out of the larger, deeper Winooski and into the Little River beginning in the middle part of September. These fish find ample gravel along the river floor to dig their redds in. Also, because the power dam frequently is in operation during the winter months and the current flow is therefore often quite high, there is relatively little chance that the brown trouts' eggs will freeze.

The migration of fish from the Winooski and up into the Little River is perhaps the most impressive attribute of this small stream. During the heat of midsummer, fish will work their way out of the Winooski, which can be over 70 degrees, to seek the comfort of the cooler waters of the Little River. Rainbows also use the Little River as a staging area for their spring spawning run.

I have taken clients into the Little River during all three seasons when trout fishing is allowed in the state. Consistently, the fish are larger and wilier than in almost any other stream I fish in this part of Vermont. This is no idle claim. I recall that during the drought of 1988, I took a husband and wife who lived in Montreal up the lower half of the Little River on a full day trip. The gentleman's wife allowed that she was perfectly content to fly-fish along the four pools immediately next to where we had parked the truck, while her husband and I ventured upstream. She claimed to have seen some very large fish lurking below a particular submerged rock ledge and wished to spend some time trying to get them to hit her assortment of dry flies.

The husband and I argued that in the heat of that day (which approached 95 degrees) it might be best to keep on the move, as the fish in any one pool would likely prove skittish. Firmly but politely, the woman assured us that she was confident of her strategy and bade us goodbye.

As the husband and I worked our way upstream, we were amazed to see many large rainbows scurrying ahead of our path. The problem was, every time we spotted a good fish, it would spook as soon as the client had placed his second or third cast over it. The client asked me to show him some alternative method of casting to these shy trout, but I fared no better than he.

Still, I was impressed by the sheer number of good fish we saw, and so was my client. He did manage to hook into two nice trout, both a bit over a foot in length. He exclaimed, as we headed back downstream to join his wife, that it was remarkable that we had seen as many healthy trout as we had, given the heat of the day and the length of the current drought. The water had been running crystal clear that year, too, causing both of us to remark that it had been a minor miracle that we had even seen a single fish all day, let alone the large numbers of 1- to 1½-foot-long browns and rainbows that had been on the water.

When we arrived at the place where the truck was parked, my client's wife was sitting idly on a rock, her waders off and her feet dangling in the water. Her husband approached her and asked if perhaps she wished to end the day's trip.

"Oh, I don't think so," she replied.

She jumped off her rock, waded through the cold water to her fishing creel, and produced a beautiful 16½-inch rainbow from it.

"It took me over an hour to get him to strike," she told us—quite smugly I might add. "But he finally took a Royal Coachman Streamer."

I think this little story accurately illustrates what it is like to fish the Little River, whether you visit it in the spring, summer, or fall. The fish are there, but you will have to show patience to get them. The water temperature, which is so much cooler than on any other stream near it, allows these fish a great advantage in survival. They will usually be active, if wary. The Little River, being a very small piece of water, allows them the luxury of being able to detect the approach of anglers and other predators. They will not be sluggish and will react quickly to any change in their domain. You must therefore use all your wiles to trip them up.

SECTION THREE

NORTHERN VERMONT

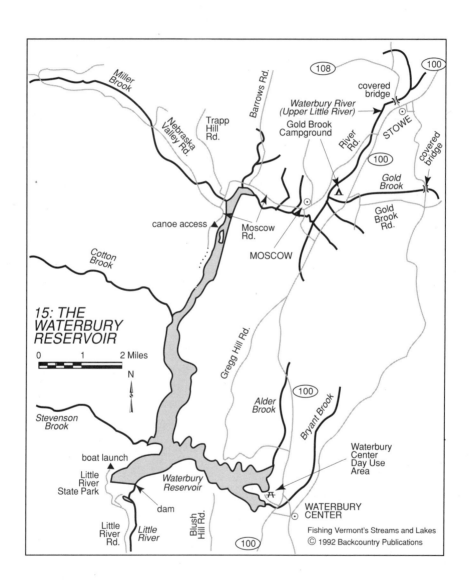

Miller Brook

108

100

covered bridge

Waterbury River (Upper Little River)

Nebraska Valley Rd.

Trapp Hill Rd.

Barrows Rd.

Gold Brook Campground

River Rd.

STOWE

covered bridge

Gold Brook

100

canoe access

Moscow Rd.

Gold Brook Rd.

Cotton Brook

MOSCOW

15: THE WATERBURY RESERVOIR

0   1   2 Miles

N

Gregg Hill Rd.

Alder Brook

100

Bryant Brook

Stevenson Brook

boat launch

Little River State Park

Waterbury Reservoir

Waterbury Center Day Use Area

dam

Blush Hill Rd.

WATERBURY CENTER

Little River Rd.

Little River

100

Fishing Vermont's Streams and Lakes
© 1992 Backcountry Publications

15

The Waterbury Reservoir

The Waterbury Reservoir is an 860-acre piece of water shaped like an upside-down Y which stretches from its northernmost point near the village of Moscow to the power dam some six miles to the south, northwest of Waterbury village. The dam was completed in 1938 after 3½ years of work and was one of four flood-damage-reduction projects built in Vermont during that decade by the Civilian Conservation Corps. The dam itself runs roughly one third of a mile in length and is over 180 feet high. The reservoir has a maximum depth of 100 feet.

In January of 1985 reconstruction of part of the downstream toe of the dam was begun to control a seepage problem that had developed. A new drainage system was put in, as were two sand-filtration systems in the toe and in the old river channel which forms the dam outflow. A new low-level outlet pipe was installed at the eastern side of the dam which allowed for a doubling of the speed with which water could be drawn out of the reservoir. This construction was completed in December of this same year.

During construction the entire reservoir was drained. Only a small trickle of a brook ran through the center of the basin. This effectively cleared out the existing populations of game fish that called the reservoir home. Since the refilling of the reservoir in 1986, the state Fish and Wildlife Department has undertaken a massive effort to repopulate it with rainbow and brown trout. In 1986, 13,200 of the Avington strain of rainbows were stocked in the reservoir, with subsequent stockings of 8,800 in 1987, 6,400 in 1988, and 250 in 1989. In 1990 Wythville and Magog strains of rainbows were stocked. These fish were all in the 10- to 12-inch range. Finally, in the fall of 1991, 1,500 large rainbows, in the 12- to 16-inch range, were stocked in various places around the reservoir. Accordingly, the state imposed a two-fish, 15-inch limit on these trout to promote their growth and to facilitate the continued monitoring of their progress.

At the same time a smaller number of brown trout were stocked in the reservoir. In 1989 and 1990, two strains of browns were stocked, the Rome and Seeforellen (1,000 of each). The Seeforellen are especially noted for their longevity and fast growth rate. There was also a large population of yellow perch which had survived in the creek left flowing through the drained reservoir during 1985. The perch have thrived since.

Creel surveys of the reservoir took place from 1986 to 1989 in conjunction with gill-net surveys from 1986 through 1991. Winter creel surveys were also conducted during 1989-1991. The results of these studies greatly surprised Fish and Wildlife personnel, as it was discovered that while the perch and brown trout were doing extremely well, the rainbow trout were showing somewhat poorer growth rates than expected. Few of the rainbows had attained the desired 16-inch-plus length. In fact a 1989 report to the Fish and Wildlife Commissioner indicated that the mean length of the Avington rainbows stocked in 1986 was only 13 inches after almost three years of living in the reservoir. Most of these 1986 fish were in the 7- to 10-inch range when they were stocked. Since 1989, though, the state has begun to stock larger rainbows with the hope that these mature fish will do better and grow faster. Stocking of brown trout continues, and these fish have attained a mean length of 21 inches in 1988 according to Fish and Wildlife Department surveys.

Waterbury Reservoir is thus an interesting fishery in that it has been built from the ground up in a very short period of time and continues to be the object of an intensive management program. Sampling of the perch, rainbow trout, brown trout, and a rapidly growing population of smallmouth bass takes place during the spring, fall, and winter. Rainbow smelt have been introduced as well, which means the major predator species, trout and bass, have been supplied with a naturally

Near the power dam, a spin-angler battles one of the Waterbury Reservoir's fine smallmouth bass while his friend readies the landing net.

occurring food source (perch) and a stocked supply (smelt). All these conditions have combined to make the Waterbury Reservoir one of the finest fisheries in the northern part of the state, with a future which could be even more exciting.

There are three access points to the reservoir. Small motorboats and canoes are easily launched at two of these sites, while the third is restricted to canoes.

The most commonly used entrance to the reservoir is located three miles to the north of where VT 100 and I-89 intersect. The Waterbury Center Day Use Area is a large open beach where families often gather for swimming, boating, and picnicking. Between Memorial Day and Labor Day, this place is filled with people, so it is best to launch your boat and get away if you intend to use this access.

There are some advantages to the Day Use Area's location for the angler in spite of its crowded nature. Alder Brook enters the reservoir in a cove just a little over a mile to the northeast of the recreation area, and it can be a very productive spot for trout and bass. Bryant Brook's mouth is located at the southern side of the point which separates the Alder Brook cove from the eastern end of the recreation area, and this can also be a good place to fish, although only during the early and late part of the fishing season. The Bryant Brook area receives intense fishing pressure during June, July, and August, not to mention traffic from all the boats and swimmers in the area.

The Waterbury Center Day Use Area is also fairly near the big point that is found across from the entrance of Stevenson Brook. Stevenson Brook is located in a small cove at the southwestern end of the reservoir. The fishing between the mouth of this brook and the outer edges of the cove can be very good during the heat of the day, as the water remains shaded throughout much of the morning. Even though the cove is at the western end of the reservoir, it is heavily shaded due to the dense growth of large trees along the shoreline. The cove itself is very narrow where it forms the mouth of the brook, and this is also one of the reasons why it is shaded for so much of the day. Stevenson Brook keeps the water in the cove cool, too, making conditions ideal for trout fishing.

The other main boat access at the southern end of the reservoir is located at the Little River State Park. This facility offers camping sites for visiting anglers, but reservations are required if you want to pitch your tent here. The park is open from the Friday before Memorial Day through the Tuesday following Columbus Day. There is a place where you can fill your tank with water, and there are numerous water faucets located throughout the park as well. For sanitary purposes the park does provide flush toilets and coin-operated showers. Lean-tos are available.

If you are making reservations for your stay at the park before May 15, you must stay a minimum of six nights; after this date, the minimum drops to three nights. The reasoning behind this policy is that it allows those people who wish to plan longer trips in advance a slight advantage in getting their reservations secured before the summer rush. For reservation information, call (802) 244-7103.

While the Little River runs through the park, the main attraction is the Waterbury Reservoir and its dam. There is a boat launch at the western end of the dam, and this is where your fishing trip will begin. During the midsummer months, people will line up along the shoreline between the launch area and the western end of the dam to fish with live bait. This is not the best way to fish this piece of water, but anglers do occasionally hook into some nice browns here during the late afternoon hours, especially in the fall. You will see other shore anglers along the eastern side of the dam from time to time, too. These folks tend to do a bit better than their counterparts at the other end, since the water runs deeper there and is shaded by a tall rock formation.

The water along the eastern side of the dam is quite deep, up to eighty feet. Deep-water trolling is the preferred method of fishing, although anglers using surface flies or top-water lures can do well during the early and late parts of the season on bass, rainbows, and browns. You will also be within easy striking distance of Stevenson Brook from this location as well as the water to the immediate north of the island.

Michael Russo, a fishing companion of mine, has perfected a simple but effective method for fly-fishing this portion of the reservoir. He will launch his canoe at the dam and paddle straight out, trolling a Black-Nose Dace streamer or a Mickey Finn weighted with a piece of split shot at a depth of about ten feet. Mike will let the wind push his canoe around the southern end of the reservoir in a somewhat haphazard manner. This seems to be a flighty method of fishing, but the erratic movement of the fly underwater as it follows the canoe does attract rainbow trout effectively.

The canoes-only access is located at the northernmost part of the reservoir, near the mouth of Miller Brook, at the end of Moscow Road, along the western shore of the reservoir. This access is blocked by a large boulder which has been placed there to prevent the launching of anything but canoes. Anglers can also hike along the shoreline for quite a distance here, as the road progresses for over a mile past the canoe put-in toward the mouth of Cotton Brook.

The fishing in this part of the reservoir is at its best during the month of May, when the rainbow trout stage their annual spawning run. The rainbows will move up into the northern end of the reservoir during this time in large numbers in an attempt to work their way into the Waterbury River. This river, which is sometimes referred to as the Upper Little River, is the main tributary to the reservoir. It extends up into the town of Stowe and boasts some good rainbow fishing of its own during the summer months.

Some of the migrating rainbows will also move into Cotton and

Miller brooks during the spring, and anglers will find that these fish, while not interested in feeding, will take a variety of artificial spinning lures and flies. Large streamers work best for fly-anglers, as these large flies will provoke the agitated fish into attacking.

During the warm-weather months of June through August, this northern area is desirable because it receives less motorboat traffic than other parts of the reservoir. The traffic situation on the reservoir is an issue which bears some discussion.

Before Memorial Day weekend the reservoir is an ideal place to paddle about and fish in. The water is cold, in the middle fifties. While some of the more avid water skiers will be found in the southern part of the reservoir, they will tend to confine their activities to the western shoreline where a slalom course has been set up. With the exception of the occasional Fish and Wildlife game warden boat, the only craft you are apt to see are recreational paddlers or other anglers in small boats or canoes. Since everyone is at the reservoir with the same purposes, enjoying the quiet and/or wetting a line, folks are respectful of each other.

Between Memorial Day and Labor Day, though, conditions change radically. As the influx of vacationing tourists picks up, boat traffic increases. During this period it is best to hit the reservoir during the very early or late parts of the day and to try to stay as far to the north of the island near Stevenson Brook as possible. This is not to say you will be unable to fish the southern end of the reservoir or the shoreline along the dam. In fact, if you work this area as soon after dawn as possible and then again just at dusk, you will find that there is little human activity present, and the fish will be active.

For two reasons, then, both the early and late parts of the season are best for fishing at the Waterbury Reservoir. Not only is the boat traffic greatly diminished, but these are the times when the major spawning runs of the smallmouth bass, rainbow, and brown trout occur. As has already been discussed, the rainbow trout stage their run in the northern end of the reservoir during May. This is a very exciting time to be fishing here, as the smallmouth are also digging their beds and mating.

The big difference between the smallmouth and rainbow runs is that while the rainbows will move in large numbers to the north and up into the Waterbury River and Miller Brook, the smallmouth tend to spread themselves all along the shallows of the reservoir's long coastline. Although during the spawning season you are not permitted to keep any of the bass you catch prior to the second Saturday in June, nor any rainbow trout under 15 inches, fishing for these two species is at its best in May.

The rainbow trout are not primarily interested in feeding at this time, although they will strike at large stonefly and caddis nymphs pulled past them at a moderate to quick retrieve. Similarly, the big Muddler Minnow can work extremely well on these fish. The secret is to recognize that spawning rainbows will attack if annoyed while they are engrossed with their annual mating ritual. This means that a dead drift is not going to be your best presentation. These fish need to be motivated, and that will require some effort on your part.

The smallmouth, however, can be provoked very easily. You will find them digging nests in the shallow shoreline areas and cruising at the drop-offs nearby. While large nymphs and poppers do catch spawning bass, your best bet at Waterbury Reservoir is to either tie a smelt streamer on your fly tippet or use a ⅛-ounce spoon lure on an ultralight spinning rig. In both cases try to place your cast close to where the bass appear to be nesting or where you see heavy growth near the shoreline. Bass like to nest near shore growth, as it provides extra shade and cover for them during the day.

Good lures to use for this task include my favorite, the Phoebe, as well as the Mepps spinner and the Kastmaster. The Mepps is a true spinning lure and as such must be handled differently from the two spoons I have mentioned. While you can buzz a Mepps along the top of a nest with good results, it is best for fishing the drop-offs. When bass lie in wait at a drop-off, they do so because the change in depth often provides them with cooler water than in the shallows as well as with a good place to hide while they keep their eyes open for a likely meal to swim by.

If you buzz your Mepps or any other type of lure with a spinner blade through the shallows and then let it stall at the edge of the drop-off, you are apt to get a strike from a hungry bass as the lure begins to fall. The action of the fluttering blade as the lure falls is quite different from the constant buzz you get when pulling your line in along the shallows at a faster speed. Bass find this irresistible.

You can use a similar technique with small, lead-weighted jigs for both smallmouth and browns. Browns will take these lures during the spring months, for they represent a very easy meal to them. I prefer using black-colored jigs and attempting to bounce them along the contours of the drop-off with a slow, irregular retrieve.

As we come into the late part of the season in September and October, the brown trout become even more aggressive. This is their spawning season, and unlike rainbow trout they will attack anything in their proximity. At Waterbury Reservoir you will find that browns will take a wide assortment of surface flies during the late afternoon hours. However, your best bet at this time of year is using weighted Woolly Buggers or just a plain old Woolly Worm, fished at varying depths and at varying speeds. I do not mean to be vague on the subject, but judging which depths and speeds work best on fall-running browns is a tricky business. These are nasty fish under the best of circumstances, so I feel it is wise not to second-guess them during this highly charged time of their calendar.

A happy angler admires a typical Waterbury Reservoir smallmouth. Note how fat this bass is. The fish was caught during the first week of October when smallmouth here engage in one final feast before winter sets in.

You can assume that if a brown sees your fly during the fall it will attack it. As you know, this is not the case during the spring and summer, when brown trout will follow a fly drifting along the surface or at a considerable depth for long distances before deciding whether or not to attack. It is really only during the early spring, just after the reservoir has iced out and when the water is beginning to warm up, and then again during the fall spawning run, that these fish lose any of their cautious nature. I find I catch almost all of the browns I get each year during these two windows of opportunity.

For equipment I suggest that you bring some of your heavier gear to the reservoir when you fish it. The smallmouth bass are often in the 3- to 4-pound range, and I have already told you how big those brown trout get. While the rainbows are somewhat shorter than either the browns or the bass, these fish are fat, much as you would expect from mature lake-dwelling rainbows. Fly rods in 5- and 6-weight are a good idea, and I would tend toward using monofilament lines in the 6-pound class for spinning gear. While there is a certain thrill to taking good-sized trout and bass on ultralight spinning equipment or a 3-weight fly rod, I can promise you there is an equal feeling of anguish that comes from losing a big brown on equipment built for much smaller fish.

One last note on the Waterbury Reservoir: from time to time the Fish and Wildlife Department conducts creel surveys. The wardens will come alongside your canoe and either ask to see what is in your creel or inquire as to your luck that day. Please cooperate with them as much as you can when they come calling. You may also come upon a Fish and Wildlife boat conducting a gill-net survey. Keep clear of the nets and the boat, as your movement in that water may disturb the department's collection efforts. The information gathered tells marine biologists about the growth of the species in the reservoir and is vital to the success the department has had in managing this fishery.

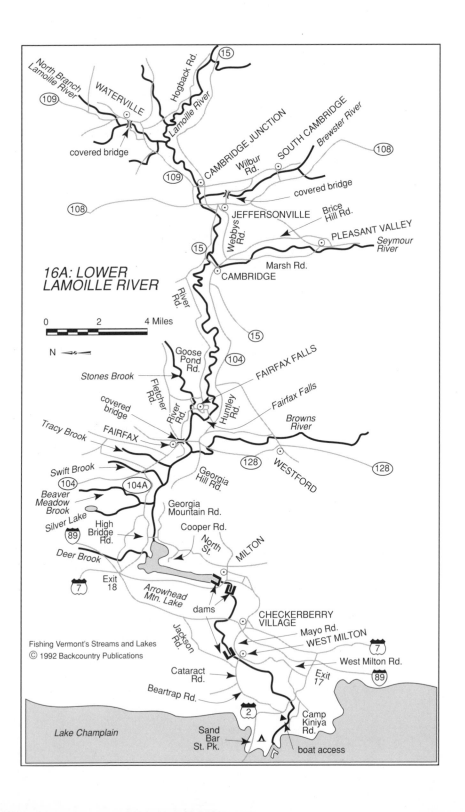

16A: LOWER
LAMOILLE RIVER

0   2   4 Miles

N

North Branch
Lamoille River

109

WATERVILLE

covered bridge

Hogback Rd.

15

Lamoille River

109

108

CAMBRIDGE JUNCTION

Wilbur
Rd.

SOUTH CAMBRIDGE

Brewster River

108

covered bridge

JEFFERSONVILLE

Brice
Hill Rd.

PLEASANT VALLEY

Seymour
River

Webbys
Rd.

15

Marsh Rd.

CAMBRIDGE

River
Rd.

15

Goose
Pond
Rd.

104

FAIRFAX FALLS

Stones Brook

Fletcher
Rd.

covered
bridge

River
Rd.

Huntley
Rd.

Fairfax Falls

Browns
River

Tracy Brook

FAIRFAX

128

WESTFORD

128

Swift Brook

104

104A

Georgia
Hill Rd.

Beaver
Meadow
Brook

Georgia
Mountain Rd.

Silver Lake

89

High
Bridge
Rd.

Cooper Rd.

North
St.

MILTON

Deer Brook

7

Exit
18

Arrowhead
Mtn. Lake

dams

CHECKERBERRY
VILLAGE

Mayo Rd.

WEST MILTON

7

Jackson
Rd.

West Milton Rd.

Exit
17

89

Cataract
Rd.

Fishing Vermont's Streams and Lakes
© 1992 Backcountry Publications

Beartrap Rd.

2

Lake Champlain

Sand
Bar
St. Pk.

Camp
Kiniya
Rd.

boat access

16

The Lamoille River

I began this book by describing the Batten Kill River as one of those streams that absolutely must be included in any guidebook of fishing in Vermont. In this chapter I will discuss another river that is just as compulsory. The Lamoille is a classic trout stream and has deservedly earned the reputation of being one of the state's premier pieces of rainbow trout water.

While I plan to devote most of this chapter to the area on the Lamoille that runs from its headwaters in Greensboro down through the township of Johnson, I would first like to give you an idea of what this stream is like as it ends. This may seem like a backward way to introduce you to the Lamoille, but bear with me. What I will give you in return is a location for a very pleasant family outing on the water.

You see, I do not get to fish on Lake Champlain all that much. Working as a fishing guide has become a full-time job for me during the summer months, and most of my days on the water are spent with clients on rivers like the Mad, the Dog, or the Winooski. So when I get a day off to fish for fun, I like to check out something new and unusual.

One summer an old friend who lives in South Hero asked me and my wife, Lauren, out for a day on the lake in his new boat. I have known John Lindsay ever since I was a kid, and he is one of my oldest friends. When he and his wife, Amy, suggested we head the boat out of their mooring and into the mouth of the Lamoille River, I was excited. If you have never fished the very bottom of this great river, a day trip by canoe or small motor boat through the last two miles of the Lamoille will make a great family trip for you.

The river runs very slowly down at the mouth, and there are several state fishing accesses available to boaters. In addition the winds that sometimes howl along the outer edge of the river's mouth are rarely a problem once you duck a couple of hundred yards into the stream. This means that even the most novice of paddlers or boaters will be able to fish here safely.

The fishing is good, especially for small and largemouth bass and panfish like pumpkinseed, perch, and rock bass. The water is usually about 6- to 10-feet deep, although there are some large, deep holes which run closer to 30 feet. Because the current is so light, it is easy to drop your lure or bait down into these holes and fish along their ledges. The rock bass are fond of these sudden drop-offs, and you should make use of a depth finder to locate the likely spots where they will be lying.

Amy did particularly well on our trip, catching two nice largemouth which she kept for dinner and about twenty-five panfish of varying sizes. I had two good-sized fish break off my 6-pound-test line after violent strikes, and Lauren caught a fair number of medium-sized fish. John, well, he had a tough day, losing many fish and missing scores of others. But then, John was having too much fun with his new boat to notice. If you pack up a nice picnic lunch and the family, drive to one of the state accesses, and launch your craft on the bottom of the Lamoille some weekend, you will have at least as good a time as we had.

But if your pleasure runs more toward wading through small streams in search of native brook trout, then you must begin your journey up in Greensboro where the Lamoille starts. Technically, the Lamoille's source is the outflow of Horse Pond, located right at the eastern corner of town. It flows down into Wheelock where it is met by Page and Morrison brooks before it turns back toward and into Greensboro again. About a mile after it reenters Greensboro, the Lamoille is met by Mud Pond Brook and Paine Brook right next to the intersection of VT 16 and Fontaine Road. This part of the river is very narrow and is best fished with a small, 3- or 4-weight fly rod. You will need to cast into some tight places to get to the brookies that live here.

After the river leaves this intersection, it flows south past two more tributaries, Edson and Flagg brooks. VT 16 runs parallel to the river on its western side. Access is not bad along here, although you will frequently have to bushwhack through some thick brush in order to get to the river. Most anglers find it easiest to start fishing at a small access right where Flagg Brook enters and to wade north to where Fontaine Road crosses the river. This is roughly a two-mile hike, so come prepared for a good, long trip if you decide to wade this stretch.

A little bit farther downstream from the mouth of Edson Brook, Gonyaw Road crosses the river. You are also within sight of another road crossing which occurs just a few hundred feet below at Young Road. Either of these bridges is a great place to take to the river. About a half-mile farther downstream, anglers will find another small bridge which also affords good access, as does the small bridge another half-mile downriver.

This grouping of tiny bridges and the one at Greensboro Bend offer anglers lots of opportunities to get at the very best fishing locations on the upper Lamoille. You will find some rainbow trout in addition to the many native brook trout as you work your way down into the Greensboro Bend area. During the fall there is also a brown trout run along this part of the river in southern Greensboro, although the real attraction still will be the brookies.

The river now enters the town of Hardwick. For its journey south until the river is met by Haynesville Brook, the Lamoille remains a small piece of water. It is still populated by brook trout, with some rainbows, and is best fished with very light gear. I found that my 7-foot, 3-inch Fenwick Iron Feather rod was perfect here. It is a stiff little 4-weight rod that allows me the luxury of a little extra power when the wind kicks up, while at the same time giving me the ability to cast into those tight spots where brookies like to hide.

The Lamoille turns to the west and begins its steady path toward Lake Champlain as Haynesville Brook enters. The river becomes wider and more exposed. This is where anglers would be well advised to break out some heavier gear, as the brown trout are in here in increasing numbers. The whole stretch that runs alongside VT 15 and into Hardwick village is good, fast-moving water. You will find some very good-sized rainbow trout in here as well.

As VT 14 and VT 15 meet in Hardwick and head up to the north, the river flows into Hardwick Lake. The lake is formed by a dam that holds back a substantial amount of water. Hardwick Lake is 145 acres, spread out over a two-mile-long valley. Anglers will find the lake

This angler often fishes the slow-moving waters of the lower Lamoille where bass like this one are quite common. While the river is best known for its rainbow trout, it hosts a wide variety of other species as well, including sheepshead, brown trout, brook trout, and pickerel.

populated by warm-water species like yellow perch, pickerel, and various panfish.

As the Lamoille heads west through Hardwick and into Wolcott, VT 15 and side roads cross it several times, providing excellent access. You will also come across a very important tributary as you enter the village of Wolcott. The Elmore Branch feeds in here, offering you the opportunity to fish its mouth for migrating trout during the spring and fall spawning seasons.

Another important feature found in the area is the Lamoille Valley Railroad line, which runs parallel to the river. As I mentioned in the chapter on the Dog River, railroad bridges can give you a unique access to any river, if you are careful. The railroad bridges on the Lamoille will also allow you to get at large brown trout by fishing around the submerged structures after the sun has gone down in the evening.

Just to the east of Wolcott village, you encounter a dam. The dam here and the one downstream from it in Morristown provide anglers with some interesting opportunities for tailwater fishing. However, some of the best fishing on this whole stretch of the river occurs just downstream from the Morristown dam near Cadys Falls.

Bill Knight is a guide who specializes in canoe fishing trips down the six-mile section of the Lamoille from just west of Morrisville through Hyde Park and into Johnson. Bill is a spin-angler, although his knowledge of this part of the river will serve fly-anglers well. He and I put his long canoe into the water during one beautiful June afternoon and set out in search of the Lamoille's famous rainbow trout.

The river is very wide along this six-mile run, although the productive pieces of water are often separated by stretches of shallow water which may extend for several hundred yards. In these shallow spots, the water is rarely more than a foot deep, and fishing is next to impossible. However, if you fish under the tree overhangs that line the shore, you can sometimes get a stray rainbow or brown to hit.

But there are plenty of good-sized holes along the way to toss your line into as well. Most of these are found along the river's many bends, and they are filled with healthy rainbow trout. Bill and I anchored his canoe at one such hole, located right at the top of the famous Ten Bends area.

The Ten Bends, a private fishing reserve, has existed on the Lamoille for many years. The owners and their members have maintained a strict catch-and-release policy along this stretch of the river. According to Vermont law, while a private landowner may restrict access to any given piece of water that runs through his property, no landowner may block or impede the travel of boats or canoes through a navigable stretch of river. This many seem confusing, but the rule of thumb is that no one may own a river itself, just the land around it.

Therefore you are allowed to keep the fish you catch in the Ten Bends area, providing you are fishing from a canoe or have reached the area by wading and do not cross the association's land at any time. Still, I recommend that all anglers comply with the catch-and-release policy. The association has created a wonderful fishing reserve on the river by enforcing the policy among its members. It seems a little bit rude to pass through and violate it as a guest. Bill and I caught seven rainbows at the top rapid at Ten Bends, all over 12 inches in length. Bill had

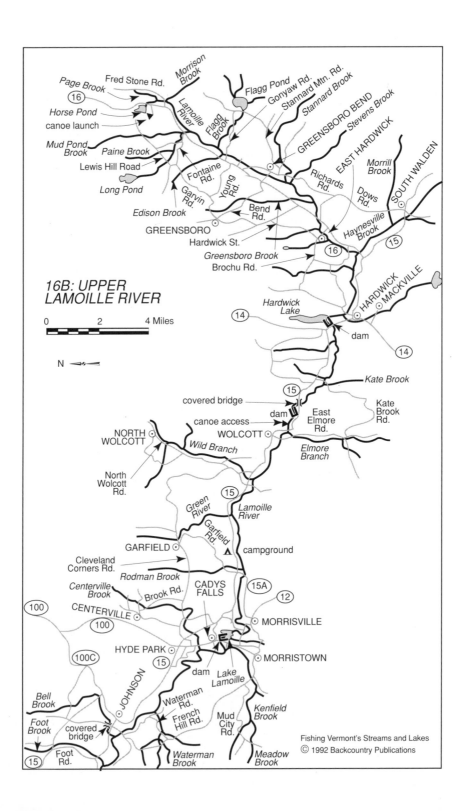

Page Brook
Fred Stone Rd.
Morrison Brook
Flagg Pond
Gonyaw Rd.
Stannard Mtn. Rd.
Stannard Brook
16
Horse Pond
canoe launch
Lamoille River
Flagg Brook
GREENSBORO BEND
Stevens Brook
EAST HARDWICK
SOUTH WALDEN
Mud Pond Brook
Paine Brook
Lewis Hill Road
Fontaine Rd.
Young Rd.
Richards Rd.
Morrill Brook
Dows Rd.
Long Pond
Garvin Rd.
Edison Brook
Bend Rd.
Haynesville Brook
15
GREENSBORO
Hardwick St.
Greensboro Brook
Brochu Rd.
16
HARDWICK
MACKVILLE

**16B: UPPER
LAMOILLE RIVER**

0   2   4 Miles

N

Hardwick Lake
14
dam
14

Kate Brook

covered bridge
15
Kate Brook Rd.

canoe access
dam
East Elmore Rd.
WOLCOTT

NORTH WOLCOTT
Wild Branch
Elmore Branch

North Wolcott Rd.

Green River
15
Lamoille River

Garfield Rd.
GARFIELD
campground

Cleveland Corners Rd.
Rodman Brook
15A
12

Centerville Brook
Brook Rd.
CADYS FALLS

100
CENTERVILLE
100
MORRISVILLE

100C
HYDE PARK
15
MORRISTOWN

JOHNSON
dam
Lake Lamoille

Bell Brook
Waterman Rd.
French Hill Rd.
Mud City Rd.
Kenfield Brook

Foot Brook
covered bridge
15
Foot Rd.
Waterman Brook
Meadow Brook

Fishing Vermont's Streams and Lakes
© 1992 Backcountry Publications

convinced me to try fishing the rapid with a spinning rod, and I caught all of my fish using a red-and-white Mepps lure.

After exhausting this pool, we pulled up the anchor and continued to drift through the Ten Bends. The edges of the shoreline held lots of smaller fish, mostly rainbows, and they all seemed to prefer to stay under the many tree overhangs during the heat of the day. The Ten Bends has many small twists and turns in it, all holding fish and all the fish falling in the 12-inch range.

Still, I was a little disappointed. You see, while the Lamoille is a good piece of rainbow trout water, it is also well known for its large browns. We had seen none of these beautiful fish, and as we left the Ten Bends, I began to wonder if we ever would. We were approaching another one of those long, dead stretches in the river, and while the water was about three-feet deep, there were no signs of fish life. There were plenty of overhangs on the southern shore, though, so I started casting at them. After several minutes, I got the strike I had waited all day for.

The fish began a furious run upstream toward Bill's end of the canoe, while also moving steadily in the direction of the southern shoreline. Bill was very excited and grabbed the landing net, hoping that he might be able to land the fish as it trapped itself between us and the shore. He used his free hand to feather his paddle in the water so as to cut off the fish's upstream angle of escape.

As we slid stern-first toward the shoreline, we got our first look at the fish. It was a good-sized brown, around 16 inches. The reason why were able to see the fish at all was because it had quickly changed direction, having sensed the presence of our canoe blocking its path. It was now headed downstream and was streaking past the canoe, only four or five feet away from us.

Bill tried to hand me the net, but I refused it. I had enough problems on my hands as it was. My fish was now about ten feet off the bow of the canoe, and it was no longer running. Instead it had begun an odd bobbing motion in the water. It would lie quite still for a second and then abruptly charge a few feet straight down. After completing this movement, it would allow itself to rise back up to its original depth and repeat the surge once again.

By bouncing up and down in this way, the trout was slowly twisting my line around and around in the water. This movement was going to cause a weakening in the line and could eventually break it, unless I could put sufficient pressure on the fish to distract it from its very effective strategy. The irritating point was that I had already allowed the fish to stretch my line quite a lot, and it was showing some sign of strain. I made one last effort to turn my fish, and it in turn made one more lunge to the bottom.

The line broke. The fish slowly began to rise back up toward the surface. After a few seconds of lying gently to one side, it flicked its tail and was gone. But I had to admit I was not terribly disappointed. I had finally seen the good brown trout that made the day complete.

Bill and I continued down the river into Johnson. The fishing here for rainbows is also quite good, and we caught and released several more. The river, as it moves downstream from Johnson into Cambridge, Fletcher, and Fairfax, is much like the section we had floated. However, once you get near the Fairfax/Milton town line, the river changes drastically. There are three dams in Milton, the first of which creates the Arrowhead Mountain Lake. This artificial reservoir is over 700 acres in size. It is a warm-water fishery and features some good fishing for smallmouth bass and northern pike. As the river feeds out of Arrowhead, it moves through the two other dams and finally empties out into Lake Champlain at the Sand Bar State Park area.

17

Caspian Lake

The small town of Greensboro is host to two great pieces of trout water: the Lamoille River and Caspian Lake. I dealt with the upper section of the Lamoille in a separate chapter so that I might concentrate here on the fabulous fishing on the lake. To get to it, you head to Hardwick, which sits at the intersections of VT 14, VT 15, and VT 16. At the Hardwick police station is a sign that points you up to Greensboro village. Follow Center Road until you hit the village. A small road that enters from your left here will lead you to the boat ramp at the southern end of Caspian Lake.

This ramp is actually at the southeastern corner of the 739-acre lake. The fishing for rainbow trout from here all the way along the southern shoreline is quite good. In the early morning hours of June and July you can see these magnificent fish rising about you as you head across the lake in search of deep water. The favored method of fishing here is trolling with downriggers, although some of the old-timers like to work lead-core line along the bottom as they hunt for the lake's most famous inhabitants: lake trout.

Caspian Lake is a deep piece of water with an average depth of 48 feet. It has two very deep holes. The one in the southern end of the lake is 142 feet deep, while the hole at the top is 120 feet. The lake trout are quite likely to be found at the very deepest portions, hiding from your lures and flies in the relative safety of these underwater depressions. However, if you have the right equipment and the proper know-how,

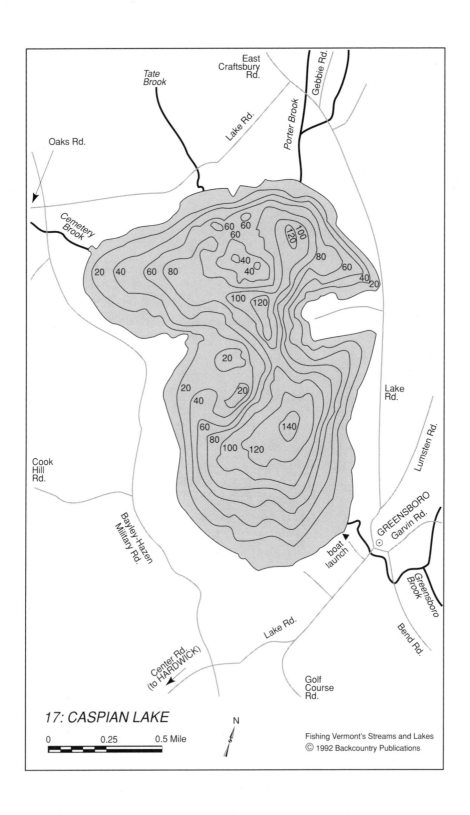

East
Craftsbury
Rd.

*Tate
Brook*

Gebbie Rd.

Porter Brook

Lake Rd.

Oaks Rd.

Cemetery
Brook

60 60
60
100
120
40   80
40   60
20 40 60 80   40 20

100 120

Lake
Rd.

20

20
20
40

Lumsten Rd.

60   140
80
100 120

Cook
Hill
Rd.

Bayley-Hazen
Military Rd.

GREENSBORO
Garvin Rd.

boat
launch

Greensboro
Brook

Center Rd.
(to HARDWICK)

Lake Rd.

Bend Rd.

Golf
Course
Rd.

17: CASPIAN LAKE

0   0.25   0.5 Mile

N

Fishing Vermont's Streams and Lakes
© 1992 Backcountry Publications

you can usually get your share of these exciting game fish.

The state has managed the lake as a salmonid fishery and has spent a great deal of time working on the rainbow and lake trout populations. Between 1977 and 1986, 25,400 lakers have been stocked, while 14,500 rainbows were stocked between 1982 and 1986. Creel surveys conducted in 1985 and 1986 show that the fishing for rainbows and lakers is good: the state estimates that 1,801 lake trout were caught during 1985, and 1,995 were caught in 1986. The estimates for rainbows are somewhat higher, with 1,577 caught in 1985 and 1,776 in 1986.

Lou Kircher has been guiding fishing trips in this part of the state for a good number of years. He guides on Seymour Lake in Morgan and Lake Willoughby in Westmore for their lake trout and salmon, but his favorite fishing spot is Caspian Lake. Perhaps this is because the lake is so close to his home in Greensboro Bend, but I truly believe the reason for Lou's affection is that Caspian is one of the most beautiful and productive pieces of trout water in this part of Vermont.

I went fishing with Lou one foggy morning in June just after the water had first warmed up to around 55 degrees on the surface. Caspian does not ice out until fairly late in the spring and often will not be fishable until the middle of May. The lake sits at an elevation of 1,400 feet above sea level, and this means that spring comes late to its waters. To give you some point of reference, the Waterbury Reservoir, which lies at about 600 feet above sea level, ices out in early April and can be fished very shortly thereafter for brown trout, rainbows, and smallmouth bass.

When Lou and I met in June, the water temperature was just right for our purposes. I brought along my Fenwick 6-weight and an assortment of streamers, while Lou carefully rigged up two spinning rods with Mooselook Wobblers. These large spoons are an irresistible lake trout lure, and he likes to fish them at depths varying from 10 to 75 feet. I told him I wanted to fish with flies and got ready to set myself up at the rear of his wood-hulled motorboat. But Lou had other plans for me and pulled out a planing board for me to use.

For those unfamiliar with this piece of equipment, a planing board is a sort of small wooden sled that you attach your fly line to with a clip. The board is then sent out to one side of the boat with an outrigger for a distance of roughly thirty feet. As the boat moves through the water, the planing board keeps your fly off to one side, away from the tangle of other lines and the motor's wake. It is best to use a sinking-tip line when fishing from a planing board. You can successfully set the hook on any striking fish by sharply pulling your rod tip upward and releasing the line from the planing board's clip. The board itself makes a fairly small wake that seems not to disturb feeding fish below.

I attached a Black Ghost streamer to my leader, rigged my line to the planing board, and we were off. The regulations on Caspian Lake, as on most lakes and ponds in Vermont, are that an angler may use up to two lines to take fish. Accordingly, Lou set out two spinning rigs for himself and another for me, just in case my fly-fishing proved ineffective. It was tough to see through all the fog, but I could hear plenty of good-sized fish rising on the water, so I was optimistic.

We set out in a series of long elliptical passes along the southern third of the lake. Depths vary a great deal in this area, from less than 15 feet all the way to 140. However, the ledges and drop-offs are gradual in this section of the lake, which made Lou's task of keeping an eye on his downriggers much easier. He kept two at 30 feet and one at 15 feet as we looped around and around in the dense fog. At one point Lou bent over for a while to work on one of the downriggers and asked me to take the helm. This was an interesting idea, as I had absolutely no idea where we were from one moment to the next. The fog was that thick. I found that my best bet was to keep my eyes on the compass and the liquid crystal fish finder in front of the wheel and to ignore my instincts as to where the land actually was. By some kind of miracle, this worked, and we successfully survived my stewardship as captain.

We were seeing fish on the fish-finder display at depths of over 70 feet, so Lou decided to head us slightly to the north, and we began the same circling motion through the middle third of the lake. Lou took back control of the wheel, and I gratefully acquiesced. The fog was still quite thick, as it often can be during the cooler spring months on Caspian. We had started our trip at about a quarter of six in the morning, and it was now almost nine o'clock. The fog was just beginning to burn off, and the air was heating up a bit too. I was now able to actually see the fish as they rose, and some of those rainbows were real monsters.

But after three hours we had not had a single strike. The planing board merrily cruised through the water to our right, but no trout had

The author shows off a laker taken from Caspian Lake on a fluorescent streamer.

seen fit to attack the streamer beneath it. Similarly, none of our three downriggers had seen any action, in spite of Lou's constant changing of the lures. He had even set out a large, multicolored streamer of his own design which was fitted with Mylar and fluorescent feathers.

The middle third of the lake is quite different from the lower section we had just fished, and we held out hope. As the lake narrows just above the exact center, it begins to taper. The span here is about 2,700 feet as compared to 4,000 feet between the two shores at the point where you find that big, 142-foot-deep hole, right at the northern end of the bottom third. There is another very large, deep hole in the middle section that extends northward all the way to the very top of the lake on its eastern side.

Just 600 feet to the west of the big hole, however, there is a rise that brings the depth to only about 20 feet. Therefore the trolling angler must keep a very steady eye on his depth reading at all times. If you are using downriggers at a depth of 30 feet or more, it is easy to run them into an oncoming shelf that you have failed to accommodate. In fact it is important to note that the entire area to the west of that deep hole at the narrows of the lake is 20 feet or less in depth.

Lou was becoming a bit frustrated with our poor luck, and as the hour moved on to eleven o'clock, he headed into the northern third of the lake. I too was impatient. As more of the lake became visible to us through the dissipating fog, we could could see lots of large rainbows feeding along the surface. I pulled in my fly line and the planing board and set up my ultralight spinning rod with a Phoebe lure. The top third of the lake is a bit more like the bottom part. As noted, a single large, deep hole of about 120 feet in depth extends through much of the eastern end. As the lake forms a cove at the eastern extremity, the water becomes much shallower and rises up to 60, and eventually less than 15 feet in depth.

To the west of the big hole there is a mound which rises up to a depth of about 40 feet before it slopes back down to around 80 feet. Then, as the western shoreline approaches, the water gradually becomes shallower again. The western wing of the upper lake is never much deeper than 60 feet.

Porter Brook and Tate Brook enter into the upper lake from the east and west respectively. We saw a large number of small rainbows rising at the outflow of Porter Brook, so I cast my lure to them. Within seconds I had a 10-inch trout on my line, and the long drought was over. Even Lou had to admit that it looked good to have at least one fish come to the boat. The time was now eleven-thirty.

A few minutes later, as we circled around the northern edge of the big drop-off near the deep hole, we got our first real strike of the day. A smallish lake trout of about 15 inches had hit one of Lou's crazy streamers and was fighting at a depth of 15 feet. Lou grabbed the line and began to reel it in.

Lou and I noticed that while we did find concentrations of lake trout feeding below the surface, we rarely saw more than four or five together at one time. By watching the fish-finder readout, we also discovered a truly astonishing bit of aquatic behavior. Two weeks prior to our trip together, the state Fish and Wildlife Department had stocked the lake with rainbow trout. These 8-inch fish were still traveling together almost the way a school of perch will. This made them very easy prey for the larger lake trout. The lakers were herding the rainbows and attacking the outer edges of their schools. According to the graph, some of these lake trout were well into the 6- and 7-pound range.

Lou dropped the downriggers to depths of 30, 50, and 70 feet. Having found such large fish in our vicinity, he was determined to hook into one or two of them. We continued to swing through the northern part of the lake, and it wasn't more than another fifteen minutes before we had another strike.

I took the rod this time, and from the very beginning, it was clear that we were into a much better fish than the first one. It had been hooked at a depth of 50 feet, so fighting it was quite a different experience from fighting the one Lou had taken at 15 feet. I had to pump the rod and was able to bring in the line only after the fish had allowed me to raise my rod tip sufficiently. It fought well, taking out line in sudden bursts as it dove away from the boat. After five minutes Lou netted it.

We caught and released several more lakers in the 16- to 18-inch range, but we never did get another fish the size of my big one. It had measured 21 inches, which is not huge by lake trout standards. Our guess was that it weighed about 3 pounds, making it a decent fish, anyway. Lou used an interesting tactic to entice the fish to strike as we trolled. He would hold our speed steady as we scanned the depths with the fish finder. As soon as we located a few good-sized fish at the depths we were fishing, he would wait until we had passed over them and our lines, which were 20 yards behind the boat, had come into the general vicinity of the trout. He would then cut the boat at a forty-five-degree angle from our course for 50 yards and then correct it again. He had found that this sudden movement made our lures and flies resemble panicked fish trying to escape the lake trout. The lakers found this irresistible and usually struck.

Fly-anglers wishing to fish for the rainbow trout in Caspian Lake might try a somewhat different line when working the water. I suggest using a canoe to work along the shoreline for the rising rainbows during the early morning hours. These fish feed on mayflies, stoneflies, and caddis throughout the morning. While their activity does subside a great deal after noon, you will still see some enormous trout splashing at the mouths of Tate and Porter brooks from time to time, even when the sun is high in the sky.

As is the case elsewhere, the Caspian rainbows stage a spawning run up the brooks during May. However, the water can often be so cold that they really are not all that interested in feeding. Spin-anglers will have a slight advantage here, especially with spinners like the Panther Martin. Bright colors seem to work well on these fish, so you should consider painting the blades of some of your spinning lures before going out on the water.

In the fall the lake trout spawn along the shallows of the lake. One of the better places to seek them out is the big mound in the northern end of the lake. Streamers work well, particularly the Black Ghost.

18

The Woodbury/Calais Lake Region

As you head northeast out of Montpelier on VT 14, you come across the lake region of Woodbury and Calais. These two communities play host to at least twenty-seven small lakes and ponds, all of them perfect for the day angler looking for some practice with his or her light gear. While motorized boats are allowed in many of these pieces of water, I urge you to fish them by canoe.

As there are so many fine places to fish here, I will attempt to describe only a few of them. I suggest, though, that you spend a good deal of time tooling around these small lakes and ponds, as they offer an enormous variety of angling opportunities.

BUCK LAKE

Buck Lake is located in the Buck Lake Wildlife Management Area, just to the north of Woodbury village and off the Buck Lake Camp Road. It is the smallest of the seven lakes and ponds to be discussed in this chapter, taking up a space of only thirty-nine acres. The state-maintained access is limited to carry-in craft, which means that only canoes can be launched. This is not altogether a bad idea, given the small size of this piece of water. The lake may also be reached by

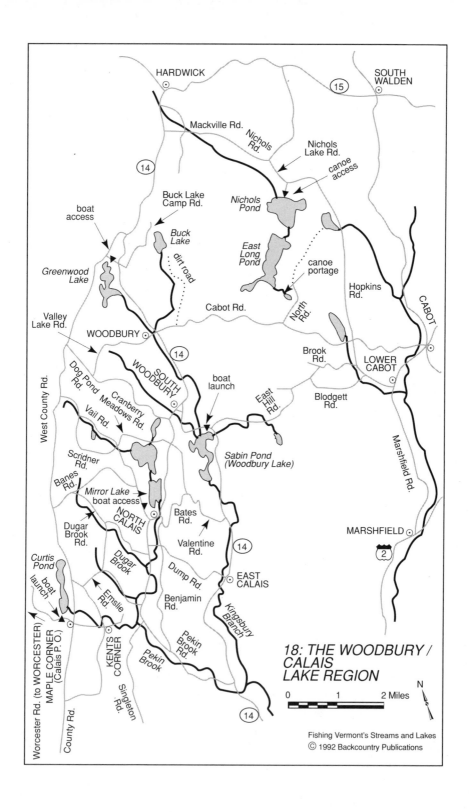

HARDWICK

SOUTH
WALDEN

15

Mackville Rd.

Nichols
Rd.

Nichols
Lake Rd.

canoe
access

14

Buck Lake
Camp Rd.

Nichols
Pond

boat
access

*Buck
Lake*

East
Long
Pond

canoe
portage

*Greenwood
Lake*

dirt road

Hopkins
Rd.

Cabot Rd.

North
Rd.

CABOT

Valley
Lake Rd.

WOODBURY

14

Brook
Rd.

LOWER
CABOT

West County Rd.

Dog Pond Rd.

SOUTH
WOODBURY

boat
launch

East
Hill
Rd.

Blodgett
Rd.

Cranberry
Meadows Rd.

Vail Rd.

Scridner
Rd.

Sabin Pond
(Woodbury Lake)

Marshfield Rd.

Banes
Rd.

Mirror Lake
boat access

NORTH
CALAIS

Bates
Rd.

MARSHFIELD

Dugar
Brook
Rd.

Valentine
Rd.

14

2

*Curtis
Pond*

Dugar
Brook

Dump Rd.

EAST
CALAIS

boat
launch

Emslie
Rd.

Benjamin
Rd.

Worcester Rd. (to WORCESTER) / MAPLE CORNER (Calais P. O.)

KENTS
CORNER

Pekin
Brook
Rd.

Kingsbury
Branch

Pekin
Brook

*18: THE WOODBURY /
CALAIS
LAKE REGION*

Singleton
Rd.

County Rd.

14

0   1   2 Miles

N

Fishing Vermont's Streams and Lakes
© 1992 Backcountry Publications

following a small dirt road that appears on the left off Cabot Road, near the center of the village.

Buck Lake is known for its smallmouth bass as well as its fine yellow perch fishing. This is a great place to use the very lightest of equipment. Small 6- to 7-foot fly rods in the 3- or 4-weight class are perfect, as is the lightest of your ultralight spinning gear. As on most bass lakes, the best action on Buck Lake is to be had just prior to the spring spawn; however, bass anglers should also check out this small lake periodically throughout the late spring and early fall. The water here warms up fairly quickly, making midsummer fishing a bit tough.

CURTIS POND

Curtis Pond is a long, skinny piece of water found near Maple Corner in Calais. The pond is small, only seventy-six acres. The state has maintained a boat launch at the southern end, which allows for canoes and small motorboats. The access near Maple Corner is easily reached via the back roads to the west of VT 14 in East Calais or by traveling east off VT 12 in Worcester.

Besides offering some good smallmouth bass opportunities, Curtis Pond also boasts some of the better largemouth bass fishing in the area. There are very few pieces of largemouth water in this part of Vermont, so Curtis Pond is unusual in this respect. Largemouth tend to congregate along the bottom of the shallow to moderate depths of the pond, and like all bass they have a definite preference for drop-offs and ledges. These fish are not colorful fighters and will rarely jump. Instead, they will make long runs toward deep water and will work to wrap your line around sunken tree limbs in an effort to snap it. They are also known for their annoying habit of seeking out exposed rocks to rub your line against. In either case the largemouth bass is a crafty prey who will make every effort to test your gear to its limit.

Most bass anglers seem to rely on ultralight spinning equipment; however fly-anglers can have a marvelous time with this species by using surface poppers and large streamers. As these bass tend to grow a bit larger than the smallmouth variety, fly-anglers may want to use 4- or 5-weight rods and 3- or 4-pound-test tippets here.

NICHOLS POND

Nichols Pond is a 167-acre body of water. It features very deep water, limited access, and some incredibly good fishing. Lake trout and rainbows are the favorite quarry of fly- and spin-anglers, especially along the western shoreline where the water runs the deepest. There is a sizable perch population as well, which tends to be concentrated along the shallows near the southern end of the pond.

The one access to Nichols Pond is for canoes only and is found off a spur of Nichols Lake Road. This piece of water is pristine and an absolute joy for fly-fishing. There is a small island located near the dam where you may launch your canoe, however, and it attracts midsummer campers. While these folks tend to enjoy the quiet of this beautiful spot, they do guarantee that you will have company on your early morning trips during the July and August vacation months.

Nichols is fantastic water for the fly-angler. Streamers are perfect, especially if you wish to lazily paddle about this lovely body of water and explore while you troll. Gray Ghosts seem to work well here, especially if they are fished deep. You will want to use your sink-tip line. You should also keep a good assortment of caddis and mayfly imitations on hand for the rainbows. Cream-Colored Cahills are plentiful on the water, particularly during June and July.

There is plenty to see too in terms of wildlife and scenery. Nichols Ledge is a striking rock formation, and all manner of aquatic birds like heron and ducks inhabit the shorelines. You may even spot the occasional moose swimming or feeding in the shallows.

GREENWOOD LAKE

Greenwood Lake is one of my favorite pieces of water in all of Vermont. Located in Woodbury right off VT 14, this eighty-three-acre lake holds a greater variety of species of fish than any other water in the state with the exception of Lake Champlain. You will find brown and rainbow trout, yellow perch, pickerel, smallmouth bass, and bluegill all over Greenwood, and in great numbers. This is a perfect spot to take a first-time angler or a child, as there is always bound to be something there that will bite.

My wife, Lauren, and I make an effort to hit Greenwood Lake several times each year. During the spring, while the rainbows may be more interested in spawning than feeding, there are usually large numbers of aggressive smallmouths that will take a nymph or a streamer. I seem to do best here using large stoneflies like a number-8 or -10 Montana, although I also do quite well using popping bugs and grasshoppers during late July and August. The type of insects you will see hatching on the surface are not all that unusual: caddis, mayflies, and such. However, you will also find a lot of biting insects like mosquitoes and black flies during June and July.

During the heat of midsummer small panfish like perch and bluegill are great fun to catch on light gear and make a fabulous meal once they are filleted. In the fall the brown trout are active and extremely territorial. I took Lauren's father, Martin, out to Greenwood one September day, and we saw dozens of 12- to 18-inch brown trout leaping and tailing. The fishing can even be quite good during Novem-

The most enjoyable way to visit the many lakes of this area is by canoe. Canoes allow anglers to sneak up on feeding trout and bass noiselessly and also provide better access to the region's many small, out-of-the-way ponds.

ber, after trout season has closed, for pickerel and bass.

There is a small-boat access on the left-hand side of VT 14 as you head east out of Woodbury village. This accommodates both canoes and small motorboats. You will find that much of the southern shore is dotted with small lake houses. The folks who live here are more than happy to share their lake with you and will even paddle out to see how you are doing. If they ask where you are from and how long you plan on staying, be advised that they are only doing this to keep track of the activity in what is effectively their backyard.

MIRROR LAKE

Mirror Lake is located right at the intersection that makes up North Calais, off Bates Road. There is a state-maintained boat access there which allows for the launching of canoes and motorboats. Mirror is another of the excellent, small, deep little lakes and ponds that cover this region. It is filled with good-sized trout in spite of its size. The entire lake takes up only eighty-six acres.

As I mentioned, this is a deep piece of water, holding rainbow trout, lake trout, and smelt. However, one thing distinguishes this lake from waters like Nichols Pond: Mirror Lake also is home to a healthy smallmouth bass population. These fish are great fun on ultralight spinning tackle as well as fly gear.

The best bets for smallmouth seem to be the usual assortment of popping bugs and heavy-hackled flies. Muddler Minnows and Woolly Buggers work well too. As some of these bass can get into the 3- and 4-pound range, you may want to use the heavier 5- or 6-weight rods.

SABIN POND (WOODBURY LAKE)

At 142 acres, Sabin Pond is one of the larger fishing spots in the Woodbury/Calais area. It is also one of the most popular. This is due to the close proximity of VT 14 and the large public launch/bathing area right off the highway. You can launch almost any kind of craft you wish to from this point, and anglers from all over Vermont hit this pond at least once in the fishing seasons in the summer and winter.

You will arrive at the pond by traveling north from East Calais along VT 14. It has a large number of small summer houses along its southern shore, and each of these homes seems to have at least one boat attached to it. As you can imagine, there is a good deal of traffic on the pond during the peak months of June through August.

My favorite time to fish the pond is the fall, for although the fishing then is not considered to be quite as good as it is in the early part of the season, there are fewer people out on the water. This gives me a much better opportunity to explore the tiny coves and shorelines for bass and trout. I may not catch as many big fish as the angler fishing in May will during the rainbow trout run, but I will catch more fish overall. There is far less pressure on this fishery in the fall, and the ever-dropping temperatures wake these fish up in a hurry from their midsummer slumbers.

You will find rainbows and smelt in Sabin Pond, particularly in early to mid-May. During the summer and into the fall the smallmouth, pickerel, perch, and bluegill will keep you amused.

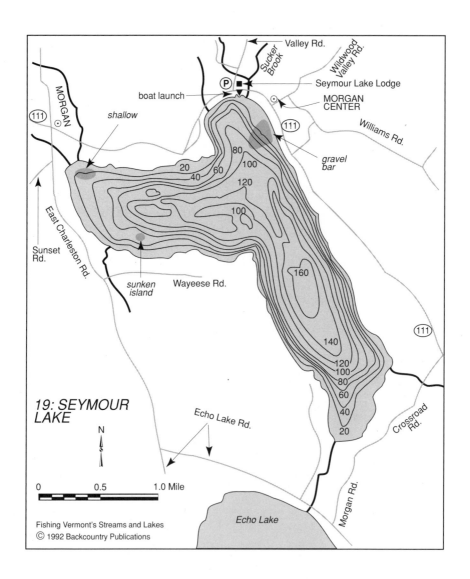

Valley Rd.

Sucker Brook

Wildwood Valley Rd.

MORGAN

111

boat launch

P

Seymour Lake Lodge

MORGAN CENTER

shallow

Williams Rd.

111

20
40
60
80
100
120

gravel bar

East Charleston Rd.

Sunset Rd.

100

sunken island

Wayeese Rd.

160

140

120
100
80
60
40
20

111

19: SEYMOUR LAKE

N

Echo Lake Rd.

Crossroad Rd.

Morgan Rd.

0   0.5   1.0 Mile

Echo Lake

Fishing Vermont's Streams and Lakes
© 1992 Backcountry Publications

19

Seymour Lake

As you head to the northeastern corner of the state, you will come upon a beautiful little town named Morgan. Inhabited by roughly five hundred people, Morgan is located on VT 111, about ten miles southeast of the city of Newport. Right in the center of the township is Seymour Lake, one of the premier fishing spots in the northern part of Vermont. The lake comprises almost 1,800 acres and has a depth of over 160 feet at one location.

If you take a ride up to the Northeast Kingdom to Morgan and wish to fish at Seymour Lake, you will find the Seymour Lake Lodge at the lake's northern end. The lodge was owned by Dan Phillabaum and his family until recently. Dan spent most of ten years exploring this beautiful piece of water.

Seymour has healthy populations of lake trout, landlocked salmon, and smallmouth bass, as well as brook and brown trout. The normal method for taking them is either to cast along the lake's vast shoreline or to cruise the circumference at low speed, trolling your baits behind you, usually Black or Gray Ghost streamer flies.

One of the best strategies is to work the area between Sucker Brook at the east end of the top of the lake and the large rock formations at the western end. I did this with Dan and his son Tod one evening in the early spring. For the first two or three hours we did not have much luck. Tod was using one of several top-water Rapala lures, while Dan and I contented ourselves with the streamers. All of us got at least one hit, but aside from the 14-inch sucker I hooked through the dorsal fin near the brook, we came up empty-handed.

Fortunately, the lake was calm, the company good, and the sky clear. It was turning into one of those pleasant afternoons where you have a relaxing time on the water and the fish do little to disturb the moment. As we neared the western rockpile for the fourth time, I switched from my fly rod to a small spinning rig and a Phoebe spoon. Two casts later I was into a healthy, if slightly undersized, lake trout. I felt the fish strike just as my lure fell off the 3-foot-deep water near the rocks into the 15-foot shelf nearby . The trout never jumped, but it did surprise me with its strength. It took me a couple of minutes to bring the fish into range where Dan was able to net it.

Tod was wide-eyed with shock. This young man has spent two-thirds of his life on Seymour Lake and was staggered when I so easily tossed my foreign lure into the open mouth of a waiting trout. Quickly he untied his Rapala and begged a Phoebe off me. Within five minutes Tod was into a somewhat larger lake trout, marveling at this new discovery. Both Tod's and my fish were under 20 inches, so we had to release them, and therein lies an interesting piece of information.

Seymour Lake is a test water. This means there are special regulations on the lake regarding fish length and creel limits. It also means the state and federal governments are closely monitoring the anglers who fish this lake. Of particular concern to this study are lake trout. You may only keep one laker per day, and it must be at least 20 inches long. Also, upon completing your day out on the water, you are required to fill out a form and register it with the state, detailing your catch or lack of one. You may only use one line per angler in your boat, too, which means no doubling up with fly and spin gear.

This creel information is part of a study of the lake. The Vermont Fish and Wildlife Department is hoping to update its own research on this important fishery. In the years 1975, 1976, 1981, and 1982, the state conducted an extensive creel survey which indicated that Seymour Lake was one of the state's better fisheries, supporting both lake trout and landlocked salmon.

The study showed that the mean length and weight for lake trout was somewhere between 20 and 21 inches and their weight in the 3- to 3½-pound range. Salmon were a bit smaller, averaging 16 to 17 inches and weighing in at about 1½ pounds. In general anglers fishing on

Gayle Phillabaum and son Tod with a lake trout taken from Seymour Lake.

Seymour Lake were more apt to catch lakers than salmon.

But there are plenty of other species of game fish living in the lake for you to pursue. Smallmouth bass populate the rocky ledges and drop-offs along the lake's northeastern shoreline. This is a fabulous area to fish crankbaits, jigs, and spinnerbaits. Fly-anglers will have great fun using popping bugs during the late afternoon hours during June and July. Fly-fishing for bass along the surface can be equally good earlier on in the season, say in May, when the smallmouth are nesting.

There is a fairly gradual series of ledges at the northeastern shore. The water drops from 5 to 20 feet fairly quickly all along this part of the lake. This is where you will find the largest concentrations of prespawn smallmouth during the spring. There are ledges a bit farther out that eventually leave you in about 60 feet of water, only about 1,000 feet from shore. The next major drop-off occurs only a few hundred feet farther out, and it brings you to depths of 100 feet and more.

The very deepest hole in the lake, however, is in the southern end, about halfway down the lower arm. This hole is over 165 feet deep, although it occurs only 300 yards from both the eastern or western shores. The water along the eastern shore is very deep, usually about 60 feet, creating a long run for anglers fishing with downriggers to cruise.

As you head up that deep channel from the south, just before you enter the big cove where the Seymour Lake Lodge sits, you will come across a remarkable underwater formation. A large gravel bed appears from the eastern shore and extends to the west into the lake, right opposite the western edge of the cove. This is actually a man-made formation, created when the state dropped large quantities of gravel and small stones onto the winter ice. The idea was to create a habitat for spawning lake trout. However, this bed can be a real hazard to navigation, especially if you are trailing downriggers. In places the water will be barely three-feet deep. Lake trout use this gravel bed as a spawning area during the fall and they will be there in large numbers through late October.

In addition to the bass you will run across a significant brown trout population. While they are somewhat scarcer than the salmon and lakers, the browns do make up a large number of the game fish available. They can grow to good size, too, as evidenced by creel surveys and local fishing reports. They will fall into the 18- to 22-inch range, healthy specimens by any standard. The average size and weight for these fish is just shy of 21 inches, and 3½ pounds.

June appears to be the best month to fish on the lake, although there can also be a great deal of activity during May. In May anglers will all wait for that first day that the lake ices out. The smelt will begin to run shortly thereafter, and this is when most anglers will first start to fish on the lake. The lake temperature can be a chilly 39 degrees just after the ice melts and while there is apt to be some activity, the best fishing will not begin until it has warmed up into the middle forties.

The lakers are the first to come up toward the surface, closely followed by the salmon. Anglers who prefer trolling do well with Mooselook Wobblers, a broad spoon lure, fished at a depth of 5 to 10 feet. These lures will have to be dropped a good 40 feet farther down once the weather warms up, so the early season is a real boon to those who like to fish closer to the top, as I do.

Fly-anglers do best by using weighted line and heavy reels. I use a Fenwick 6-weight rod which measures out to 8½ feet. The extra length proves to be very helpful as I prefer to fish this piece of water by canoe. The fish that occasionally rise at the surface can be easily spooked, so the extra 10 or 15 feet of line I can cast out with my rod can often make the difference between success and failure.

I also make sure I bring two reels, one filled with a floating line and the other with a sinking-tip. Since these two types of line take up very different amounts of space on the reel, I make sure I have a large enough reel for either. For example, when I went fishing with Dan and Tod, I was using a Berkley 556, which does a good job of holding either the bulky floating line or the sleeker sinking-tip as well as 50 yards of backing material.

Not to get too involved in products, if you are planning on spin-fishing for the long-running species like landlocked salmon, you should also consider the type of reel as well as selection of lure, line weight, and so on. Some reels will only provide you with a 4.5- or 5-to-1 gear ratio. A big salmon is likely to run a great deal of line out of your reel while you fish it and is just as likely to rush at you once it has finished that run. When the fish does this, it helps to have a reel which can help you bring in your line in a hurry. I've been using the Shimano Symetre reels and have found that they offer an enormous advantage to the angler when this happens. The Symetre features a 6-to-1 gear ratio, which affords me a little more breathing room when I hook into a big fish out on the lake.

One last advantage which proper selection of equipment can bring you on Lake Seymour has to do with the craft you plan on using. While motorboats do allow the angler to move about this big lake freely and at great speed, I again urge you to use a canoe. In the chapter on fishing tactics early in this book, I explained that canoes give you greater stealth in your approach. What I did not mention there was how little friction your canoe offers as it plows through the water. A good-sized bass, trout, or salmon can very easily pull your canoe through the water as it runs. This puts a little less pressure on your fishing line than it would have to bear if you were in a larger, heavier motorboat or if you were fishing from the shore. Use this factor to your advantage, and have the person fishing with you steer you around as you follow the fish. This can be especially helpful should your fish try to head toward sunken logs, stumps, or other obstructions. Your companion can gently head the canoe back into open water with a far subtler motion that any motorboat can.

Seymour Lake is most easily reached via VT 111, which runs between Island Pond to the south up to its northernmost point in Derby Center. Since most of the land surrounding the lake is privately owned, I recommend that you park in the lot across from the Seymour Lake Lodge and launch your boat or canoe from the beach across the street. (Note: In May of 1992, Dan Phillabaum sold the Seymour Lake Lodge. It is now owned and operated by Sue and David Benware.)

20

The Clyde River

I have always held that VT 100 is the most beautiful road in the entire state of Vermont. It certainly brings you through some of the state's most interesting country.

VT 100 begins its northward journey in Stamford, at the Massachusetts/Vermont border. It takes you alongside the White River, the Mad River, the Winooski, the Lamoille, the Missisquoi, and many other great pieces of fishing water not discussed in this book. Once it ends, just to the west of the city of Newport at the intersection of VT 100 and VT 105, right under the Canadian border, the visiting angler is met with one of the most remarkable sights and experiences to be found anywhere in the state.

Newport is located on the southern shore of Lake Memphremagog, a large body of water which Vermont shares with the Province of Quebec. Here anglers fish for healthy populations of walleye, bass, and trout either from motorboats or canoes. During the winter, ice shanties spring up all around the frozen lake's surface. However, by far the most exciting and unusual events to take place on the lake are the annual spawning runs of landlocked salmon, rainbow trout, walleye, and bass up the tiny Clyde River on the lake's southeastern shore.

The fishing along the lower Clyde is very difficult but also extremely rewarding. The prime area to fish starts on the upstream side of the Clyde Street Bridge by the power dam owned by Citizens Utilities and extends about a mile downstream to the US 5/VT 105 causeway. The

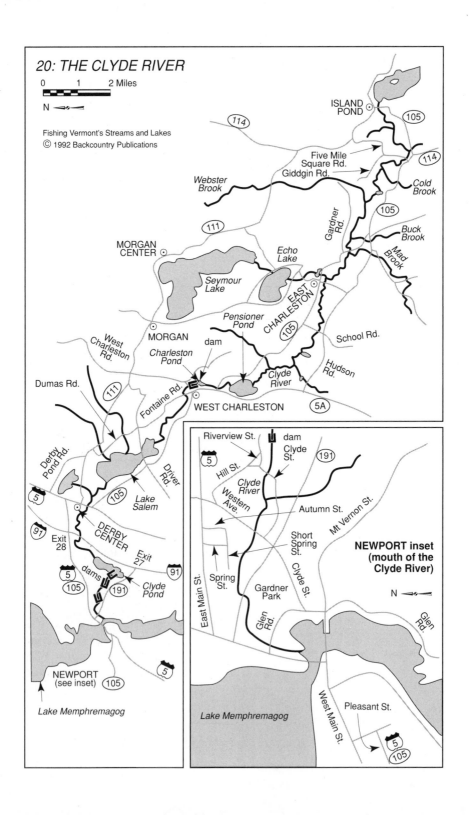

20: THE CLYDE RIVER

0   1   2 Miles

N

Fishing Vermont's Streams and Lakes
© 1992 Backcountry Publications

ISLAND POND
114
105
114
Five Mile Square Rd.
Giddgin Rd.
Cold Brook
Webster Brook
105
Buck Brook
111
Gardner Rd.
Mad Brook
MORGAN CENTER
Echo Lake
Seymour Lake
EAST CHARLESTON
105
School Rd.
Pensioner Pond
MORGAN
dam
Charleston Pond
West Charleston Rd.
Hudson Rd.
Clyde River
Dumas Rd.
111
Fontaine Rd.
WEST CHARLESTON
5A

Derby Pond Rd.
Driver Rd.
5
Lake Salem
105
DERBY CENTER
91
Exit 28
Exit 27
91
5
105
dams
191
Clyde Pond
NEWPORT (see inset)
105
5
Lake Memphremagog

NEWPORT inset (mouth of the Clyde River)

Riverview St.
dam
Clyde St.
5
191
Hill St.
Clyde River
Western Ave.
Autumn St.
Mt Vernon St.
Short Spring St.
East Main St.
Spring St.
Gardner Park
Clyde St.
N
Glen Rd.
Glen Rd.
Lake Memphremagog
West Main St.
Pleasant St.
5
105

river is very narrow, perhaps only fifty yards across at the widest point. It also runs with almost no surface interference, as there are few large obstructions or narrows to cause rapids and runs. This piece of the Clyde is one long, skinny pool with an average depth of only four or five feet.

The tranquil water conditions allow fish a perfect opportunity to scrutinize every bait that floats past them. Anglers using minnows and worms will have a field day with the river's large yellow perch population and will also catch a few nice bass on the side. However, they will have a very tough time with the salmon and the trout. These fish, which average in the 3- to 5-pound range, are extremely wary and will follow your offering for long stretches before deciding whether or not to strike.

As the lower Clyde is a well-known fishing spot to most anglers living in the Newport area, things can get a little crowded along the banks, particularly after five in the afternoon. But here's the most interesting point of all: there is a set code of conduct followed by all who visit the Clyde, a code which seems to work perfectly for everyone.

By custom, fly-anglers tend to fish the farthest upstream and will begin to line up along the southern shore, just downstream from the Clyde Street Bridge. The first fly-angler in line will wade halfway across the river and begin casting to the northern shoreline for a few minutes. After five or ten minutes, this angler will move forty or fifty feet downstream, and the next one in line will move into the space. This process continues until everyone has had a chance to pass through the hundred yards or so of this prime fly-fishing water. While the fly-anglers are wading here, the spin-fishermen will work the water below, using a similar system which does not involve wading. In this way everyone gets the same opportunity at the fish.

The fish, for their part, don't seem to be disturbed by this activity. Spin-anglers using a variety of jigs, spinning-blade lures, and spoons will be into bass and other warm-water fish all day, while the fly-anglers will work the spawning trout and salmon. Every so often an angler will let out a shout as he or she hooks into a huge salmon or rainbow, and all the other anglers will stop what they're doing to watch. It's a very supportive and enjoyable way to fish, for everyone gets in on the action in one way or another.

Anglers have the most success on the Clyde salmon and trout using streamer flies, although I have also had a couple of good fights using light spinning tackle and Phoebe spoons while fishing the river with guides Mike Olden and Dean Wheeler. However, the streamers did seem to produce the best results. Several patterns produced strikes, but none was more effective than the Black Ghost. This fly is fished both at a dead drift and pulled in a jerking motion against the current. Most anglers got their strikes while retrieving the Black Ghost back against the current, with the fly weighted down by a small piece of split shot.

I met Mike Olden and Dean Wheeler during the winter of 1990–91 while researching this book. Mike owns a roadside tackle shop in Newport and spends as much of his free time out on the water as possible. You will find this to be the case with most fishing guides. Even though their work hours are spent showing visitors the local streams and lakes, days off are usually forays into new waters or return trips to familiar fishing holes.

Mike and I met to fish one May afternoon when the clouds were just beginning to break up for the first time in a week or so. The weather in this northernmost outpost of the Vermont fishing world can be very harsh during the spring months, and it is not unusual for snow as well as heavy rain to spoil a fishing trip during the late-April to mid-May period when the big spawning runs occur. I had driven up from my home a few hours early to sneak in a little while on the water alone and had lost a good-sized salmon on a Woolly Bugger at about three in the afternoon.

Mike joined me at about five-thirty with a beautiful custom rod he had made from a Fenwick blank. It was an 8-weight rod, but it actually weighed a few sixteenths of an ounce less than my Fenwick Iron Feather 6-weight. Both rods were exactly 8½-feet long, but the material used to make Mike's made it lighter to work with.

We headed to a spot on the river where the state of Vermont had posted signs declaring a 100-yard stretch to be off-limits to anglers between the first Sunday in April and the second Saturday in May. Anglers may only fish between the hours of 5:00 A.M. and 8:00 P.M. EST or 6:00 A.M. to 9:00 P.M. EDST during this period and may only fish with a single, unweighted hook. This means no treble rigs, although streamers and wet and dry flies with a single hook are perfectly legal. The area from the dam downstream to just shy of 300 feet below the Clyde Street Bridge is prime nesting water for the spawning salmon and the state has worked to protect this area from overfishing through this restriction. A similar restriction exists during the fall on this part of the river, allowing for only catch-and-release fishing with artificial lures and flies.

Mike was wearing chest waders, which gave him access to the widest part of the river, right at the top of the portion where fishing was allowed. He waded into the water and began casting toward the northern shoreline a Black Ghost streamer that had been tied by Dean Wheeler. After a few minutes a shout went up from one of the fly-anglers just downstream, near where I was fishing. A two-foot rainbow trout was moving into the area where Mike was fishing. We all watched from along the southern shore as the big trout rose again and again, moving steadily toward Mike.

"It won't make much of a difference, y'know," an angler to my right told me. "Those fish may rise like all hell, but that really doesn't mean they'll strike at anything."

I puzzled over this for a few seconds, and then I heard another shout. This time it was Mike, and his big Fenwick rod was doubled over as though he'd just hooked bottom. However, the rod tip was also bouncing up and down and the line whizzed out from Mike's reel as the fish zigzagged through the water downstream. All the other fly-fishermen stopped casting and watched as Mike battled his fish.

"Oh, God!" he exclaimed as he first got a look at it. It was a huge salmon, and it ran sideways to the north shore before turning sharply again downstream. That was when Mike's 4-pound tippet gave out. With one last frantic lunge, the salmon broke off the end of the leader and escaped with Mike's fly in its mouth.

The epilogue to this fish story is a fun one. The following night one of Mike's friends caught a 7½-pound landlocked salmon on the same piece of the Clyde we had fished. The fish put up a tremendous fight, and after it was landed, a brand new Dean Wheeler Black Ghost was found in its jaw, right alongside the streamer the angler had used to catch it. The Black Ghost was presented to Mike the next afternoon.

Since Dean Wheeler's flies figure so prominently in this last tale, I should tell you more about him. Dean is a fine fly-tier, as well as being one of the nicest people I have ever had the pleasure to fish with. Dean's favorite Clyde River fly, the Black Ghost, is a specialty of his, and his work is in great demand from fly-fishing shops throughout the

northern portion of Vermont for his variations on this and other classic
salmon and trout patterns.

Dean and I met about a week after my trip with Mike to fish the
Clyde. The restrictions on parts of the river that could be fished had
been lifted, so I spent some time upstream from the Clyde Street Bridge
fishing the outflow of the power dam there. While I could still see
salmon moving into the area below the dam, it was clear that most of
the activity I had seen just a few days before was ebbing. I tied on
several different streamer patterns, including a Mickey Finn and a Gray
Ghost, but could not get the fish to respond.

Returning downstream to where Dean was fishing, I noticed that
spin-anglers were doing quite well on what appeared to be an invasion
of smallmouth and rock bass. Clearly the absence of the salmon and
trout had made way for the spawning bass. Two anglers were having
particularly good luck on small Rapala lures, fished at a depth of about

Michael Olden casts his streamer downstream to spawning landlocked
salmon on the lower Clyde River. Five minutes after this picture was
taken, Mike laced into a beautiful fish which snapped his four-pound
tippet. So it goes ....

two feet along the shoreline they stood on. They would alternately cast up or downstream, allow the lure to settle for a few seconds, and then retrieve it as close to the shore as they could.

The shoreline of the Clyde features a very sudden drop-off. The rocky bottom provides a multitude of places for fish to hide, and the bass were all lying close to this shelf, among the larger rocks. I switched from the Black Ghost I had been using and tied on a Gray Ghost pattern adorned with a few pieces of olive green feather. My hope was to imitate the various species of small minnow I had observed congregating flush up against the bank.

Dean came over to watch me as I cast upstream, right along the near shoreline. I was aiming at the rings where I had just seen a fish rise.

"I don't think that's going to do you much good," he observed quietly. "For some reason, the sighting of a rise doesn't really help you in getting it to strike."

Dean smiled pleasantly and sat down to watch some more. This was the second time in as many weeks I had received this piece of advice about fishing on the Clyde, but I was determined to prove it false. After fifteen minutes of casting to the rising fish, and after changing my fly and retrieve more than a dozen times, I had to agree with it, though. While I flailed madly at the water, the fish continued to rise merrily without a single acknowledgment of my efforts. I turned away from it and headed downstream.

About 100 yards below where I had been casting the was the Newport State Highway (VT 191) bridge, which links VT 5 with I-91. I hiked down and under the bridge and began to cast once I was about 50 yards downstream from it. Almost immediately, I got a hit. About a minute later, I pulled in a healthy foot-long rock bass.

The rock bass has two interesting characteristics. The most famous are its red eyes. Known as the goggle eye by many anglers, the rock bass is not particularly prized either by sportsmen or meat fishermen. I had observed one old-timer earlier that day as he angrily cursed each rock bass he caught just prior to disdainfully tossing it back into the river. On the other hand, I have always found that the rock bass can put up a fairly good fight on a fly rod. You see, the second characteristic of this fish is its broad body, which it expertly turns into the current and away from the angler, using its slightly curved bulk to resist the pull of the line. In this way the rock bass puts up a much tougher fight than other species its size and weight. Granted, you will rarely see a rock bass take to the air after being hooked, but I feel this is more than made up for by the fish's surprising strength. I spent about an hour fishing for rock bass downstream from the bridge. After a while they stopped hitting, and I walked back to find Dean.

I found him sitting on an old abandoned dinghy which had been left overturned, engaged in an animated conversation with another angler who was bending over the water's edge fiddling with something. Dean is one of those fishermen who is equally happy talking about fishing as casting to a rise, and it is this peaceful attitude which I find most appealing about him. The other angler was just finishing a story when I walked up, and Dean turned to me and made a quick introduction.

"This guy just caught quite a nice bass, Pete. You should take a look at it," Dean said, pointing to his new friend.

The other man said nothing, but smiling broadly, he reached down into the water where he had been kneeling and lifted a huge, 4-pound smallmouth from the bank where he had been reviving it. After allowing me to take a few pictures, he put the fish back into the water, and we watched it swim away. It is legal to catch and release bass on the Clyde between the second Saturday in April and the second Saturday in June, however it is not permitted for an angler to keep these fish during this two-month period. The state allows bass a healthy amount of time to build their beds and spawn on them before meat fishermen may prey on them.

Another angler, one of the two I mentioned who were using Rapalas, was now into a fish, and while it turned out to be just a scrappy one-pound smallmouth, the aerial display the fish put on made it fun to watch. None of us caught a salmon on that day, although we did spot several fish in the 20-inch-plus range working along the northern shoreline. The spring salmon and rainbow run on the Clyde usually lasts a few weeks and can occur during the last week of April through most of May. As mentioned, you are also apt to find spawning bass in this same piece of water, usually toward the middle of the salmon run through the month of May.

The rest of the Clyde should be explored, as well as the lower reaches. There are two more hydroelectric dams between the one near the mouth and Clyde Pond. The water here is relatively flat and slow moving, but you can run into some awfully nice rainbows in the tailwater. Clyde Pond itself is a warm-water fishery and is best known for its smallmouth bass. Bass will run from Clyde Pond all the way through the part of the river which winds through Derby township, although you will also find some good rainbows from about Derby Center upstream to Lake Salem. Access is good, and you will find lots of pools and riffles to cast to. The wading is not too tough, either.

Following the river upstream to Charleston Pond, you will find mostly a rainbow fishery. There is a hydro site at the pond itself, providing you with good tailwater to fish. If you continue upstream, you will come upon increasing numbers of rainbows and eventually even populations of native brook trout when you get close to the Clyde's source at Island Pond.

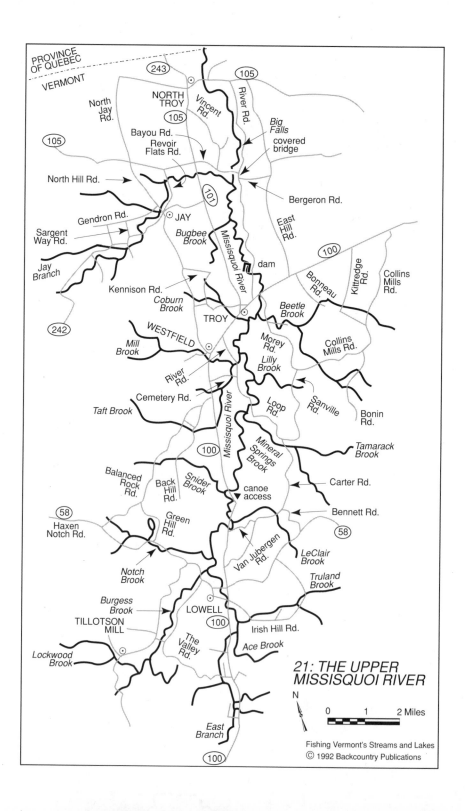

PROVINCE OF QUEBEC

VERMONT

243

105

North Jay Rd.

NORTH TROY

Vincent Rd.

River Rd.

105

105

Big Falls covered bridge

Bayou Rd.
Revoir Flats Rd.

North Hill Rd.

101

Bergeron Rd.

East Hill Rd.

Gendron Rd.

JAY

100

Sargent Way Rd.

Bugbee Brook

dam

Bonneau Rd.

Kittredge Rd.

Collins Mills Rd.

Jay Branch

Kennison Rd.

Coburn Brook

TROY

Beetle Brook

242

WESTFIELD

Morey Rd.

Collins Mills Rd.

Mill Brook

Lilly Brook

River Rd.

Cemetery Rd.

Loop Rd.

Sanville Rd.

Bonin Rd.

Taft Brook

100

Mineral Springs Brook

Tamarack Brook

Balanced Rock Rd.

Back Hill Rd.

Snider Brook

canoe access

Carter Rd.

58

Green Hill Rd.

Bennett Rd.

58

Haxen Notch Rd.

Van Jubergen Rd.

LeClair Brook

Notch Brook

Truland Brook

Burgess Brook

LOWELL

TILLOTSON MILL

100

Irish Hill Rd.

Lockwood Brook

The Valley Rd.

Ace Brook

21: THE UPPER MISSISQUOI RIVER

N

0   1   2 Miles

East Branch

100

Fishing Vermont's Streams and Lakes
© 1992 Backcountry Publications

21

The Missisquoi River

The Missisquoi River is a large piece of water in every sense of the term. Its full length is seventy-four miles from its beginnings in Lowell to its mouth in Lake Champlain. We are going to limit our discussion of this fine trout river to its uppermost reaches as it passes from Lowell to Westfield to Troy and finally on into Quebec.

This is a unique stretch of water. Very little research has been done on it by the state Fish and Wildlife Department. Most of the efforts of the state fisheries biologists in this part of Vermont go toward keeping an eye on lake trout in places like Seymour Lake, Lake Memphremagog, and Lake Willoughby. Seymour is a test water and is discussed in Chapter 19.

Local anglers will tell you of the fabulous brown trout fishing on the upper Missisquoi. Mike Olden, a guide who works the Clyde River and Lake Memphremagog, has spent years fishing on the Missisquoi. He claims the best time to fish this large river is during the early fall, right when the brown trout have started their spawning run.

The river is formed by the drainage of a large number of small tributaries in the southern part of Lowell township. Lockwood, Ace, Truland, Notch, and LeClair brooks all feed into the headwaters of the river. In fact the river technically begins only where it hits the Lowell/ Westfield town line, just east of Browns Ledges.

You will see this early portion of the river from VT 100, on the western side of the road. The river is at its narrowest here, although it is still a fairly good-sized piece of water. Brook trout inhabit the mouths of the various streams that make up the headwaters, but you will find brown trout in the main stem of the Missisquoi. These fish are not huge, but you will find some in the 12-inch range. This part of the river is best during the spring, when water levels are at their highest. You will also find the fishing quite good during the fall when the browns and brookies spawn.

There are several good holes in the short twisting stretch of the river at the very northern part of Lowell. These should be fished with care, as they hold the largest of the trout you will find here. Various fly patterns work well, including caddis, Hare's Ear, and mayfly. Dry-fly-anglers will want to wait at least until after the first week or so in May before fishing here, as the water takes a while to warm up sufficiently. During the late spring and on into the first week of July, though, the fishing for brookies and browns can be quite good, and you will also be able to use attractor patterns like the Royal Coachman or the Ausable Humpy.

Snider Brook enters the main stem from the west just after the river begins its flow into the town of Westfield. Immediately afterward the river turns sharply to the east and away from VT 100. Between here and the village of Troy, some six miles north, you will find the prettiest and most exciting fishing on this whole upper section of the river.

The river winds for over three miles through remote countryside until it runs under the bridge at Loop Road. There are not too many riffles or rapids in this stretch, although there are some good, deep holes for big browns to hide in. The slow pace of the river here is in contrast to the Missisquoi in Lowell, which does have some fast-moving water. The payoff in the section between VT 100 in Westfield and where the highway crosses again just east of Troy are the big fish and beautiful scenery.

This part of the Missisquoi gets little attention from most anglers, mainly due to the fact that access to the river is so hard to come by. Your best bet is to spend some time traveling up and down VT 100 asking landowners for permission to cross their land to get to the water. You should also take this opportunity to ask them what they know about the water which runs through their backyards.

I have spent some time in an earlier chapter discussing the rules of etiquette regarding landowners and using the rivers that run through their property. There is a new rule that needs to be brought up right now as it pertains to this portion of the Missisquoi River. A monastery is located along the shores of the Missisquoi in this particular piece of the river. The residents are very sheltered people who have withdrawn from the world at large by their own choice. Folks who live in the Westfield and Troy area have told me that they choose not to fish the shore here, as they feel it is an infringement on the monastic community.

There is, however, a perfectly logical way to preserve privacy for the monastery and get at the good fishing in the river. During the spring months the Missisquoi runs quite high, and it is possible to put a canoe into the river down at the Lowell/Westfield line where VT 100 crosses the river. You can then float the whole six-mile stretch downstream to where VT 100 crosses the river once again. I would caution you that the Missisquoi runs very low during mid-July through August. This makes canoe trips almost impossible through this area at that particular time.

As you paddle through the Missisquoi on your springtime trip, though, you will find that the river is fed by several more tributaries. Mineral Springs, Lilly, Taft, and Mill brooks are the largest of these. In fact you can even get to the river by hiking down Mill Brook from an access point near Westfield, right on VT 100. Mill Brook itself is an excellent piece of brown trout water and should be explored carefully.

There is also another way to get to the river toward the end of this six-mile run. Cemetery Road and River Road both intersect VT 100 from the east and head toward the Missisquoi. River Road actually heads south and crosses the river twice. The same road also intersects Mineral Springs, Lilly, and LeClair brooks. An awfully nice stretch of river, which can be waded, runs between a bridge on the lower half of River Road (where it turns into the Loop Road), and a small spur off River Road near Westfield. Be careful, though. There has been a problem with erosion on the Missisquoi, so the bottom can get get muddy. You would do well to either fish with someone who knows the area or to fish with a partner close by to help you in case you get into trouble.

As for the many brooks that feed the main stem of the river, I suggest that you spend some time investigating them for brook and brown trout, but they should be fished only during the early and late seasons.

Huge pools like this one are the norm on the Missisquoi River. The depth of this one is over ten feet.

In the spring the water from the snow runoff keeps the levels in the smaller tributaries to the Missisquoi very high. As the main stem is apt to be a torrent during April and early May, the best fishing along this area is on the brooks rather than in the river itself. However, once you get into June and early July, both the river and the brooks can be equally good fishing. The problem you will have is deciding which is more fun on any given day. Both the brooks and the river will have enough water in them to keep the fish population happy. This in turn will offer you an abundance of opportunities.

By mid-July, though, the brooks will have started to dry up somewhat. As August heats up, the brooks will be reduced to a trickle, and fishing in them will be next to impossible. The main river will be tough going, too, but not if you seek out the less traveled, more heavily shaded sections. The Missisquoi becomes a nighttime angler's river during this time of year. Big browns can be caught at twilight and on into the evening on Leadwing Coachman, Hare's Ear, and stonefly nymphs.

As the weather begins to cool during September and the rains return, the fishing along both the brooks and the river's main stem picks up again. Caddis flies, Light Cahills, and Adams flies are among my favorites for this time of year, although I also swear by various streamer patterns. The Black Ghost and Muddlers work well.

Getting back to the river below Westfield, Coburn Brook enters the main stem near the intersection of VT 100 and VT 101, right at the village of Troy. If you stay on VT 100, River Road will enter on the north side of the road. This road offers you about ten miles of good access to the river, all the way up to where VT 105 intersects near North Troy village.

The first point of interest in this stretch is the dam that appears about a mile after you turn off VT 100 and onto River Road. There is a parking area, and anglers can fish either up or downstream from here. There are large, deep pools on both sides of the dam which attract swimmers and other anglers during the warm summer months. You may want to hit these pools yourself with a sinking-tip line early in the morning during June and July. The brown trout fishing can be especially good here during the evening hours.

Some folks may even want to try to launch a canoe here and ride the river the six miles down to the covered bridge at Bayou Road. There are a few tricky rapids to be negotiated, particularly during the early part of the season. Lots of twists and bends in the river create a good number of deep holes for you to work with wet flies and streamers. You will also notice that there are many large trees along the river banks, casting long shadows on the water during the late afternoon. In fact the light disappears quickly on this stretch of the river once the sun goes down, so I would not advise starting this trip too late in the day. There are few hazards in the water to bother you, but it is far better to keep things on the safe side. Early morning trips will work well along here, as the brookies seem to prefer feeding then, anyway.

If you do want to try this stretch of the river in the evening for the fine brown trout fishing, I suggest that you explore River Road in a four-wheel-drive vehicle and stop along the two-mile piece just below the dam to fish. There are plenty of good places to pull over, and most landowners will grant you permission to cross their fields if you ask ahead of time.

The river turns sharply away from River Road after this point and winds its way toward the confluence with Bugbee Brook. The fishing from this point all the way north to the covered bridge is outstanding, but access is very tough. There will be times when you will feel sure that you have completely lost the river. But if you remember that it is always on your western side, you will be able to figure out where it is through the fields and trees. At one point the river is almost a half-mile to the west of the road.

Once you get to the covered bridge, though, things become much easier. While the river does drift away back to the west by several hundred yards from time to time, for the most part you will have a lot less trouble than before in getting to it from River Road. In fact, if you start wading at the bridge and work your way downstream, you will pass through a beautiful section of the river which receives very little pressure at all. You are going to have to commit yourself to this little hike, however, because it will be almost a mile before you find a good place to climb out of the river and back onto the road.

About two miles downstream from the covered bridge, you will come upon one of the truly great attractions of the Missisquoi River. Big Falls is a fifty-foot cliff which the river washes over as it heads into a lovely gorge below. The fishing for big brown trout in the gorge and the outflow of the huge rapid below it is fabulous. You will want to have that extra spool of fly line ready when you fish here, as you will need to switch from floating to sinking-tip line to get at the bottom of the very deepest pools.

Big Falls is a well-known swimming and picnicking area. During the summer months you are apt to run across sizable crowds of people enjoying the water and scenery. However, if you make your own visit after five in the afternoon, many of the sun-worshipers will have already left. As in all high-walled gorges, the sun disappears quickly here, leaving the sunbathers with dark, chilly shadows instead of the warm light they came for.

The water downstream from the falls and the big rapid is fabulous, too. You are now very close to the border that Vermont shares with Quebec, but you will be able to find some good brown trout in the remaining stretch of river. The one area where you will have to be careful is about 1½ miles beyond Big Falls. The river opens up a great deal here, and the shoreline gets quite mucky. Footing is poor, and I certainly would not advise fishing it unless you can do so with a guide or with someone else who is familiar with the place.

22

Beaver Pond Brookies

Among my favorite places to fly-fish for trout are the many small beaver ponds which cover the more remote forest locations of Vermont. Some of these ponds are as small as a few hundred square feet, about the size of the first floor of most people's houses. Others may cover several acres. However, these small pieces of water can offer an angler some of the best fishing around.

Beaver ponds are formed when a family of beavers blocks off the flow of a mountain stream with tree limbs, mud, and other debris. A large pool is quickly formed just upstream from the dam, and as it widens and deepens, the beavers will work to expand the dam's size. Eventually the stream backs up and floods the surrounding terrain, creating the pond.

The fish most apt to inhabit these tiny streams where the beavers work their engineering magic are native brook trout. The brookie is a native to the state and can be found in almost every cool, running stream. However, once they are trapped by a newly constructed beaver dam, they become the property of the pond it forms, and they thrive.

Brookies survive well in beaver ponds because while they continue to received cold, oxygenated water from the upstream flow, they enjoy a greatly expanded food source as a direct result of the formation of the pond. While they lived in the tiny stream that preceded the pond, these brookies had to compete heavily with each other for the limited number of emerging aquatic insects and the nymphs that lived along the stream floor. However, now that their brook has been transformed into a pond with a much larger surface area and greater depth, the number of insects that hatch, emerge, and lay new eggs will increase to an almost infinite quantity.

Most of these beaver pond brook trout will fall into the 6- to 8-inch range. The reason why most of them are so small is the same as the reason they are usually quite small when we find them in the upland streams. Brook trout are exceedingly prolific, and it is the competition for food and oxygen caused by their sheer number that limits their growth. However, some of these pond fish will grow rapidly and exceed lengths of a foot. I have caught and released brookies in the 12- to 14-inch range when fishing in ponds scarcely more than a thousand square feet in size.

Finding productive out-of-the-way beaver ponds to fish is not always easy. Many of the ponds that are most readily accessible to us by car or foot receive steady fishing pressure and as such are sometimes devoid of trout. Still, these ponds can produce plenty of enjoyment for the angler searching for a quick hour or two of relaxing fun at the end of a day at work. When the mayflies begin to hatch in the early morning or late afternoon on a spring day, and those small brookies start to feed on them, a tranquil beaver pond can be transformed into a dramatic spectacle. There can be as many as several hundred trout rising at the same time on some of the larger ponds I've fished. Hooking into one of them is as easy as casting to a grouping of rises and allowing your fly to rest on the water's surface for a few moments. When brookies feed like this, they are not all that selective, and they will hit almost any offering.

But sometimes an angler feels the need to explore new territory and to seek out larger, more challenging fish. This is when a little research can pay off.

Perhaps the best tools for this project are the aerial photographs supplied by the Vermont Department of Property Valuation and Review. These photos show in fine detail the terrain of every township in the state and make locating remote ponds and streams very easy. To get the photos for the area you would like to explore, consult the Vermont Mapping Project division. They will send you a map of the state, broken up into quadrants, requesting that you identify according to a grid system the area you would like to see in detail. Each aerial photograph costs fifteen dollars and will be sent to you about a week after your request is received. You reach the Vermont Mapping Project by writing to 43 Randall Street, Waterbury, Vermont 05676.

The aerial photos are also available at every town hall in the state, but the photographs will only cover the land inside that single township. If you already know which towns you would like to fish in, check the maps at the appropriate town halls and take note of the identifying numbers at the bottom of the page. Then, when you order from the Mapping Project, you will have the reference information you need to speed your request along.

Beaver ponds show up quite well on these aerial photographs, but you are going to need one more tool to make your search for out-of-the-way ponds successful. Once you have located a grouping of beaver ponds on the aerial photographs you obtained from the Mapping Project, you will need to cross-reference their location with nearby roadways and logging roads. The U.S. Geological Survey has produced

Beavers will begin by damming up a small stream like this one. In time, the entire surrounding area will flood, creating the pond.

topographic maps of every part of the state, and these maps are available at most outdoor outfitting shops. The maps are extremely valuable, as they will show you where the ponds you are interested in are in relation to prominent landmarks. Mountain peaks, valleys, and streams can all be used as points of reference as you hike to your remote beaver pond.

I've also found that the maps supplied by the Vermont Department of Transportation can be helpful in offering likely landmark information. You will need a good compass, too, if you are to accurately track and cross-reference all these resources. You might also place a call to a local land-development firm and ask if they are aware of the ponds you have located on your aerial photos. They may be able to provide you with time-saving information on the location of logging roads or hiking paths that lead into the area you wish to reach.

Often the beavers will find small flows of water that are little more than springs and create some very elaborate dam systems out of them. They will also do repair work on abandoned dams. I've seen dams which have had several feet of new construction on them, salvaging the old, crumbling structure. Beavers are very powerful animals and can chew and pull huge amounts of timber through dense forest to strengthen the dam that holds their pond together.

They can also make fishing very difficult for you.

Being territorial and inquisitive creatures, beavers will investigate any disturbances in their backyards. When a beaver notices someone mucking around the shore of its pond, or climbing along the top of its dam to get a better vantage point on some rising trout, it may decide to swim out to investigate. Trout, being somewhat less bold than this large swimming mammal, will tend to get out of the beaver's way when it comes to look you over. When the beaver swims into your casting range, many of the rising trout will disappear. If you are lucky, the beaver will swim back and forth in front of you a few times and upon deciding you are innocuous will return to whatever it was that it was doing before it noticed you. The brook trout are apt to return to their feeding activity in just a few minutes. On the other hand, if the beaver determines you are either a threat or a nuisance, it will continue its sentrylike patrolling in front of you until fishing becomes impossible and you leave.

Should you continue to ignore the animal's implied request that you depart, it will often circle in close to you and, with a dramatic flourish of its bulky tail, dive and thrash its tail violently on the water. This will clear out even the bravest of trout from a hundred-yard radius of where you stand. The sound of a beaver beating its tail can be heard for quite a distance and resembles the Warner Brothers cartoon sound effect of a boulder falling from a great height into the water far below.

If you are lucky, the beavers will not be at home, and you will be left alone to fish without disturbance.

The brook trout I've encountered in most Vermont beaver ponds are not as selective as their stream-dwelling cousins. They seem to strike at moving objects more often than stationary ones, and they show a preference for flies or lures which are fished just a bit below the surface. This is not to say that a delicately placed Elk Hair Caddis won't do the trick when the air temperature runs in the mid-seventies during June and July. However, a number-16 Montana nymph or a similar-sized Woolly Bugger seems to work best when stripped in at a brisk pace three to six inches below the surface. If you find the fish aren't hitting your fly but persist in striking at everything else that moves on the water, slow down your retrieve a bit.

It helps to keep your eyes on the water for changes in fish behavior, insect hatches, and other aquatic animals. As most astute trout anglers know, all three of these factors are closely interrelated. If you notice the trout are rising full out of the water, you are apt to see insects buzzing around the water's surface, just emerging from the slick on top of the pond. Likewise, if you see that the fish are swirling in the water just a few inches below the surface, check for the presence of nymphs and emergers fighting their way up to the slick.

There are other things to look for, too. During the latter part of June and into July, check around the edges of the pond, particularly in shaded areas, for signs of brook trout fry. These tiny fish, normally less than an inch in length at this time, are a sure indicator that the pond you are fishing has a very healthy population of trout living in it. Salamanders are also a welcome sight, as their presence points to a pure water supply.

I find that I have significantly better luck at setting the hook on a striking beaver pond brookie when I keep my rod tip low to the water and hold the rod at about a thirty-degree angle to one side of the direction of my cast; in other words, if my cast is at twelve o'clock, I

There is perhaps nothing as relaxing and therapeutic to the mind as casting to rising brook trout on a beaver pond.

keep my rod at either ten o'clock or two o'clock. Brookies strike in a peculiar sideways fashion, and hitting back at them from this slight angle helps my ratio of set hooks versus missed strikes considerably. Hooking brook trout found in streams is a little different, as the natural flow of the current does all sorts of strange things to your line and your fly, forcing you to strike on your fish in a straight up-and-down motion to take best advantage of the fish's downstream escape. However, when you fish the placid surface of a pond, you will find this little trick quite helpful.

You see, the brookie will follow your fly until it is sure that it is something to eat. Then it will move straight in on the target, but at the split-second before it meets the fly, it will turn from its head-on attack mode and onto its side, beginning a dive for the bottom. Because brookies attack in this way, they tend to miss the fly quite often, so don't be too hard on yourself if you don't hook up on your first few strikes.

One very frustrating day a few years ago, I was missing brookies right and left on one of my favorite ponds when I noticed something quite bizarre. As I watched yet another eight-incher escape, I realized that these fish were jumping full out of the water around my fly and attempting to take it as they came back down into the water. The next fish that struck at my line flew high into the air, but I suppressed the urge to set the hook until I saw the trout come back down. As the fish's head broke back into the pond, I pulled my rod tip back and drove the hook home.

The fish fought quite hard, and when I brought it in, I noticed with some embarrassment that I had actually foul-hooked it through the tail. I released it and made my next cast. A few seconds later another fish leapt over my fly and began to fall back again toward the water, its mouth wide open. I struck at this fish as it hit the surface and fought it in successfully. To my horror this fish was hooked neatly through the tail as well! I can only assume that both of these fish actually missed my fly on their downward attack and that sheer luck had allowed them to be caught. The odds against catching two fish in this way must be astronomical, but I caught and released several more, hooked through the tail, before I left the pond that day shaking my head in disbelief. Each of these trout had jumped over the fly, tried to take it on the free fall, missed it, and gotten hooked in the derriere for its trouble (all such foul-hooked trout must be released).

When you are out fishing for beaver pond brookies, you are apt to get many more strikes than you might normally enjoy on even the most productive of trout streams, if conditions are right. Moderate air temperatures, in the sixties or seventies, no wind, and water-surface temperatures in the high fifties to low sixties seem to be best. When you come across a pond which lies mirrorlike in the woods with nothing disturbing the surface except for the dimples of fish rising, you might take the opportunity to make a few experiments with your technique.

One might be to question the way you set the hook. A good friend of mine from New Hampshire, Paul Manseau, told me to try a strange little trick he employs. As described above, hold the rod tip in the air at about a thirty-degree angle from the surface of the water as you retrieve the fly. When you see the fish hit, instead of pulling *up* on the fish, sharply *drop* your rod tip toward the water and then slowly bring it back up again. Oddly enough, when you drop the tip, the line will jump toward you, and the barbed end of the hook will tend to drive itself upward. This means that you will be more likely to hook the fish in the upper jaw than the lower, eliminating the possibility of injury to the fish while you fight it. It takes a bit of practice to suppress the instinct to pull up on the strike, but you might find this tip very helpful if you are out for a quiet morning of catch-and-release fishing.

You will need a fairly light rod to cast to these beaver pond brookies, say a 6½- or 7½-foot, 3- to 5-weight rod with a double-taper floating line. I use a 4-weight, 7½-foot graphite rod with an extra spool of weight-forward line. This allows me to switch to the faster-loading weight-forward from my double-taper line, should the wind pick up on the pond where I'm fishing.

You will want to wear a pair of hip waders, as the mud around most ponds and dams can be quite deep, and you will also want to be able to wade out on those parts of the pond which will support your weight. As ponds grow older, an increasing amount of silt deposit is pushed toward the dam by the upstream flow. This silt can be treacherous for wading anglers, and you should tread carefully at all times when you step off solid ground into the water or the tree branches which make up the dam. It's very easy to become stuck in the sediment and muck.

Almost any fly will work on beaver ponds, but besides the Montana and the Woolly Bugger, there are a few patterns which seem to be especially successful. Brightly colored attractors like the Royal Wulff or Yellow Humpie are my favorite dry-fly patterns, and you also shouldn't forget the Black Ant and the Cricket for midsummer casting. Sometimes, if there is little or no activity on the surface, a Cricket weighted down with a small piece of split shot can be deadly. In all of these cases, though, you would be well advised to choose fly sizes in the number-16 to -20 range. Brookies have fairly small mouths, especially if they are in the 6- to 10-inch range, which makes up most of the population of the beaver ponds you are most apt to fish.

Index

Ace Brook, 185
Alder Brook, 137-138
Andover, 29
Arlington, 41
Arrowhead Mountain Lake, 152

Baldwin Creek, 105, 106
Bartlett's Falls, 102-103
Bartonsville, 30
bass season, 19
Batten Kill River, 35-42, 145
    equipment suggestions, 37, 39,
      40, 41
    management of, 38
    map of, 36
    origin of, 35
    stocking of, 38
Beaver Brook, 101
beaver ponds, 191-198
    equipment suggestions, 198
    locating, 192
beavers, 194-195
Berlin, 95, 96
Bethel, 63, 69, 70
Big Falls, 190
bluegill, 107, 164, 165, 167
Bolton, 123
Braintree, 69
Bridgewater, 51, 54
Bridgewater Corners, 54, 56
Bristol, 101, 103, 107
Broad Brook, 56

Brockway Mills, 31, 33
Brookfield, 70
Brook trout
    fishing technique, 195-196,
      197-198
Browns Ledges, 185
Bryant Brook, 138
Buck Lake, 161, 163
    equipment suggestions, 163
Bugbee Brook, 189
bullhead, 119
Butternut Bend Falls, 49

Cadys Falls, 149
Calais, 161, 163
Cambridge, 152
canoe fishing, 22-25, 174
    strategy, 22-24
Caspian Lake, 153-160
    depth of, 153, 156, 158
    lake trout, 153
    map of, 154
    population studies, 155
    stocking of, 155
catch-and-release fishing, 16-17
    flies and, 20-22
    how to, 17
    injured fish and, 22
    lures and, 20-22
Charles Folsom Brook, 87
Charleston Pond, 183
Chateauguay Brook, 56

Chelsea, 70
Chester, 29, 31
Chester Depot, 30
Clay Brook, 84
Clyde Pond, 183
Clyde River, 175-183
    code of conduct, 177
    equipment suggestions, 178
    map of, 176
    special regulations, 182
Coburn Brook, 189
conservation, 16
Cota Brook, 101
Cotton Brook, 139, 140
creel surveys see also population
    studies
Curtis Pond, 163
    equipment suggestions, 163

Derby, 183
Derby Center, 183
Deweys Mills Pond, 58
Dog River, 91-99, 120
    conservation and, 99
    equipment suggestions, 96
    map of, 92
Dorset, 35, 45
Dowsville Brook, 89
Dufresne Pond, 37

East Calais, 167
East Granville, 69
East Randolph, 70
East Rupert, 45
Edson Brook, 146, 147
electroshock surveys see popula-
    tion studies
Elmore Branch see Lamoille River
equipment, 25
    fly rods, 25
    line, 25

planning board, 155-156
reels, 25
spinnerbaits, 114-115
tippet material, 25
equipment see also individual
    waters

Fairfax, 152
fallfish, 121
fishing seasons, 19
Flagg Brook, 146-147
Flower Brook, 46
Freeman's Brook, 81

Gassetts, 30, 31
Gaysville, 69
Granville, 62, 63, 66, 68, 81
Green River, 41
Greensboro, 145, 146
Greensboro Bend, 147
Greenwood Lake, 164-166
guides, 15-16

Hancock, 62, 63, 66, 68
Hardwick, 147, 153
Hartford, 51, 57, 59, 63
Hartland, 51
hatches
    black flies, 83, 113, 165
    caddis, 59, 71, 113, 165
    caddis flies, 47
    cahills, 47, 85, 164
    Dobsonflies, 59
    hellgrammite, 59
    mayflies, 48, 59, 71, 83, 113,
        123, 165
    mosquitoes, 83, 113, 165
    stoneflies, 47-48, 59, 71
Haynesville Brook, 147
Herrick's Cove, 32, 34
Hinesburg, 107

Horse Pond, 146
Hyde Park, 149
Hydroelectric dams
    fishing and, 32, 127-128
    fishing upstream from, 32

Island Pond, 183

Johnson, 145, 149, 152
Joiner Brook, 124

Lake Memphremagog, 175, 185
Lake Salem, 183
Lake St. Catherine, 50
Lake Willoughby, 185
Lamoille River, 144-152, 153,
    175
    Cadys Falls, 149
    Elmore Branch, 148
    equipment suggestions, 146,
        147
    Lower, map of, 144
    origin of, 146
    special regulations, 119
    Ten Bends, 149
    Upper, map of, 150
largemouth bass, boating of, 112
LeClair Brook, 185, 187
Lewis Creek, 107
Lilly Brook, 187
Lincoln, 101, 102
Lincoln Brook, 81, 83
Little Mad Tom Brook, 35
Little Pond, 50
Little River, 122, 123, 125-131,
    138
    map of, 126
Little River State Park, 138
Lockwood Brook, 185
Lowell, 185, 186, 187
Lower Granville, 62

Mad River, 81-90, 175
    development of, 86
    equipment suggestions, 84-86
    map of, 82
    origin of, 81
    Punchbowl, The, 86
    stocking of, 88
Mad Tom Brook, 35
Manchester, 35
Manchester Center, 45
maps, 14-15
Mettawee River, 43-50
    Butternut Bend Falls, 49
    management of, 43
    map of, 44
    origin of, 45
    population survey, 43
Middlebury, 73
Middlebury Gorge see Ripton
    Gorge
Middlebury River, 73-80
    map of, 74
    Middle Branch, 73
    North Branch, 73
    origin of, 73
    South Branch, 73
Middlebury River see also Ripton
    Gorge
Middlesex, 81, 120
Mill Brook, 50, 81, 87, 187
Miller Brook, 139, 140
Milton, 152
Mineral Springs Brook, 187
Mirror Lake, 166
    equipment suggestions, 166
Missisquoi River, 175, 184-190
    Big Falls, 190
    Browns Ledges, 185
    equipment suggestions, 186,
        188-189
    map of, 184

origin of, 185
special regulations, 119
Montpelier, 97, 120
Moretown, 81, 89, 90
Morgan, 169
Morrison Brook, 146
Morristown, 149
Moscow, 135
Muddy Branch *see* New Haven
    River
Mud Pond Brook, 146
Murphy Brook, 101

New Haven, 101, 103
New Haven River, 101-106
    Bartlett's Falls, 102-103
    management of, 104-105
    map of, 100
    Muddy Branch, 104, 106
    origin of, 101
    population studies, 105
New Haven River Anglers
    Association, 104
Newport, 175
Nicholas Pond, 164
North Calais, 166
North Duxbury, 123
northern pike, 50, 107, 109, 112,
    115, 119, 152
    feeding habits, 115
Northfield, 93, 95, 98
Northfield Falls, 95
North Royalton, 69
North Rupert, 46
Notch Brook, 106, 185

Orvis, 31
Ottauquechee River, 51-59
    equipment suggestions, 58-59
    map of, 52-53
    North Branch, 54, 56

origin of, 51
population study, 54, 56
Quechee Gorge, 58
stocking of, 59
Otter Creek, 73, 101, 106
    special regulations, 119

Page Brook, 146
Paine Brook, 146
Patterson Brook, 62
Pawlet, 45, 46, 49
perch, 107, 119, 163, 164, 165,
    167, 177
photography, 16
pickerel, 164, 166, 167
Pine Brook, 88
Pinney Hollow Brook, 56
Pittsfield, 68
Pleiad Lake, 73
Pond Brook, 107, 109, 112
Porter Brook, 158, 160
Poultney River, special regula-
    tions, 119
Punchbowl, The, 86

Quebec, 175, 185
Quechee, 58
Quechee Gorge, 58
Quechee Gorge State Park, 57

railroad bridges, fishing near, 97,
    148-149
Randolph, 69, 70
Ripton, 73
Ripton Gorge, 75-77
    access to, 76, 78
    equipment suggestions, 76-77,
        78
Riverton, 95, 96
Rochester, 63, 66, 68
rock bass, 181-182

Rockingham, 29
Roxbury, 91
Royalton, 63, 70, 71
Rupert, 45

Sabin Pond, 166-167
salamanders, 195
salmon, Atlantic, 66, 69
    description of, 72
Salmon Hole, The, 117
salmon, landlocked, 117, 169,
    173, 177
Sand Bar State Park, 152
Sandgate, 41
Seymour Lake, 168-174, 185
    equipment suggestions, 171,
        173
    map of, 168
    population studies, 170-171
    spawning area, 172
    special regulations, 170
Sharon, 63, 71
Shepard Brook, 81, 88, 89
Sherburne, 51
Sherburne Center, 51, 54
smelt, 136, 166, 167
Snider Brook, 186
South Randolph, 70
Stamford, 175
steelhead, 117
Stetson Brook, 81, 83
Stevenson Brook, 129, 138, 139,
    140
Stockbridge, 63, 68
Stony Brook, 37
Stowe, 139

Taft Brook, 187
Taftsville, 57-58
tailwater fishing, 128
Tate Brook, 158, 160

Ten Bends, 149
Trout Brook, 29
Trout Hollow, 84
trout season, 19
Troy, 185, 187, 189
Truland Brook, 185
Tunbridge, 70
Tweed River, 68

U.S. Geological Survey, maps,
    193-194
Upper Little River see Waterbury
    River

Vermont Department of Property
    Valuation and Review, 192
Vermont Department of Trans-
    portation, 194
Vermont Fish and Wildlife, 19
Vermont Fish and Wildlife
    Department, 43
Vermont Mapping Project, 192-
    193

Waitsfield, 81, 87
walleye, 117, 119, 123
Warren, 81, 84, 102
Warren Falls, 83
Washington, 70
Waterbury, 120, 121, 123, 128
Waterbury Center Day Use Area,
    137-138
Waterbury Reservoir, 125, 127,
    134-143
    equipment suggestions, 141-
        143
    map of, 134
    population studies, 136, 143
    stocking of, 135
Wells Brook, 50
West Arlington, 41

West Bridgewater, 51, 54, 56
Westfield, 185, 186, 187, 189
West Hartford, 71
West Woodstock, 57
Wheelock, 146
White River, 59, 62-72, 175
    equipment suggestions, 71
    First Branch, 70
    map of, 64-65
    population studies, 63
    Second Branch, 70
    special regulations, 72
    stocking of, 66, 72
    Third Branch, 69
    West Branch, 68
White River Junction, 63, 72
White River Valley Camping
    Area, 69
White River Wildlife Management
    Area, 71
Williams River, 28-34
    Andover Branch, 29
    Herrick's Cove, 32
    map of, 28
    Middle Branch, 29, 31

origin of, 29
South Branch, 31
stocking of, 31
Williams River State Forest, 29
Williamstown, 70
Winona Lake, 107-116
    equipment suggestions, 109-
        110
    map of, 108
    poison ivy, 115-116
Winooski River, 90, 117-124,
    125, 127, 128, 130, 175
    equipment suggestions, 123-
        124
    map of, 118
    Salmon Hole, The, 117
    special regulations, 117-119
Wolcott, 149
Woodbury, 161, 164
Woodbury/Calais Lake Region,
    161-167
    map of, 162
Woodbury Lake *see* Sabin Pond
Woodstock, 51, 56, 57

Also from The Countryman Press and Backcountry Publications

The Countryman Press and Backcountry Publications, long known for fine books on the outdoors, offer a range of practical and readable manuals on fish and fishing for sportsmen and women.

Bass Flies
> by Dick Stewart, $12.95 (paper), $19.95 (cloth)

Fishing Small Streams with a Fly Rod
> by Charles R. Meck, $14.95 (paper), $24.95 (deluxe cloth edition)

Flies in the Water, Fish in the Air: A Personal Introduction to Fly Fishing
> by Jim Arnosky, $10.00

Fly Tying Tips
> edited by Dick Stewart, $9.95

Good Fishing in the Adirondacks: From Lake Champlain to the Streams of Tug Hill, Updated, edited by Dennis Aprill, $15.00

Good Fishing in the Catskills: From the Waters of the Capital District to the Delaware River, Second Edition, by Jim Capossela, $15.00

Good Fishing in Western New York: The Finger Lakes and Other Waters, from Oneida Lake to Chautauqua Lake, edited by C. Scott Sampson, $15.00

Ice Fishing: A Complete Guide...Basic to Advanced
> by Jim Capossela, $15.00

Orvis Guide to Beginning Fly Tying
> by Eric Leiser, $9.95

Our Native Fishes: The Aquarium Hobbyist's Guide to Observing, Collecting, and Keeping Them, by John Quinn, $14.95

Pennsylvania Trout Streams and Their Hatches
> by Charles Meck, $14.95

Taking Freshwater Game Fish: A Treasury of Expert Advice
> by Todd Swainbank and Eric Seidler, $14.95

Universal Fly Tying Guide
> by Dick Stewart, $9.95

Virginia Trout Streams: A Guide to Fishing the Blue Ridge Watershed
> by Harry Slone, $14.95

We publish many more guides to canoeing, hiking, walking, bicycling, and ski touring in New England, the Mid-Atlantic states, and the Midwest. Our books are available through bookstores and specialty shops. For a free catalog on these and other books, please write The Countryman Press, Inc., Dept. APB, P.O. Box 175, Woodstock, Vermont 05091.